CRATER LAKE

THE STORY OF ITS ORIGIN

List of References

ALLEN, J. E.
  1936. "Structures in the Dacitic Flows at Crater Lake, Oregon," *Journal of Geology,* Vol. 44, pp. 737–744.
*ANDERSON, TEMPEST, and FLETT, J. S.
  1903. "Report on the Eruptions of the Soufrière, in St. Vincent, in 1902," *Royal Society of London, Philosophical Transactions,* Ser. A, Vol. 200, pp. 353–553.
ATWOOD, W. W. JR.
  1935. "The Glacial History of an Extinct Volcano, Crater Lake National Park," *Journal of Geology,* Vol. 43, pp. 142–168.
CHANEY, R. W.
  1938. "Ancient Forests of Oregon: A Study of Earth History in Western America," *Carnegie Institution of Washington Publication No. 501,* pp. 631–648.
DILLER, J. S., and PATTON, H. B.
  1902. "Geology and Petrography of Crater Lake National Park," *U. S. Geological Survey Professional Paper No. 3.*
*LACROIX, A.
  1904. *La Montagne Pelée et ses éruptions.* (Paris)
MERRIAM, J. C.
  1933. "Crater Lake: A Study in Appreciation of Nature," *American Magazine of Art,* Vol. 26, pp. 357–361.
MOORE, B. N.
  1934. "Deposits of Possible *Nuée Ardente* Origin in the Crater Lake Region, Oregon," *Journal of Geology,* Vol. 42, pp. 358–385.
  1937. "Nonmetallic Mineral Resources of Eastern Oregon," *U. S. Geological Survey Bulletin 875,* pp. 155–166.
*PERRET, F. A.
  1935. "The Eruption of Mt. Pelée, 1929–1932," *Carnegie Institution of Washington Publication No. 458.*
SMITH, W. D., and SWARTZLOW, C. R.
  1936. "Mount Mazama: Explosion versus Collapse," *Bulletin of the Geological Society of America,* Vol. 47, pp. 1809–1830.
WILLIAMS, HOWEL
  1941. "Calderas and Their Origin," *University of California Publications, Bulletin of the Department of Geological Sciences,* Vol. 25, pp. 239–346.

* These papers describe the glowing avalanches of Mont Pelé.

newly formed, crossed by red-hot tongues of lava and choked with hissing fumes; and those fateful days when showers of glowing ash laid waste the land all round, and the summit of the mountain, with deafening noise, collapsed into the depths. We imagined an earlier time, when the volcano was sheathed in ice and pierced the clouds while wintry blasts swept across its shoulders; and when, in angry mood, it blew giant clouds of steam and pumice high into the upper air while torrents of foaming lava gushed from its sides. We recalled more distant days, before Mount Mazama existed, when dense, tropical forests covered the land, and ages even more remote, when the waves of an open sea rolled over Oregon. Seeing these panoramas pass in the mind's eye, we turned once more to look between the hemlocks and gaze on the lake with a deeper appreciation of its majesty.

afterward. Certainly, hundreds of animals must have perished when the avalanches raced down from Mount Mazama, and perhaps a few Indians also were overwhelmed. By chance, tomorrow or the day after, erosion or excavation may uncover their bones."

We thanked him for his kindness, and left. Next morning was to be our last in the park. We rose to watch the dawn from the rim. Soon the western wall was aglow with brilliant light. For a long time we sat among the hemlocks watching the constant play of shadows on the water, entranced by the beauty of the changing scene. In the deeper parts of the lake the color was indigo and Prussian blue. In the shallower places it graded to turquoise blue. While the lake lay placid and the sky was cloudless, the blues mingled with the browns and reds reflected from the cliffs. A breeze stirred the water; the reflections vanished, whitecaps ran in streaks across the blue, and golden bands of pollen blown from pine trees made winding patterns. The sky filled with clouds, and the blues disappeared, submerged in leaden grays. Hardly a moment passed without some transformation.

> Their colors and their forms, were then to me
> An appetite; a feeling and a love,
> That had no need of a remoter charm
> By thought supplied, nor any interest
> Unborrowed from the eye.
>
> WORDSWORTH, *Tintern Abbey*

After a time, satiated with visual delight, our thoughts turned back to earlier scenes. We pictured the caldera,

As we rose to leave, one man said, "I've been told that Indians were living near here when the mountain disappeared. Can you tell us if that is true?"

"There is no doubt about it," was his reply. "A few years ago several pits were dug along the banks of the Deschutes River, near Wikiup. While the workmen were digging, they found some large, well-made knives of volcanic glass or obsidian in a layer of glacial material overlain by pumice blown from Mount Mazama. Later, Professor Cressman and a party of students from the University of Oregon excavated a small cave near Paisley, about 80 miles east of Crater Lake. There again, Indian relics were found buried under pumice. Among the relics were part of a sagebrush bark mat, some sagebrush rope, a little basketry warp, the butt end of a spear thrower, and several stone scrapers. None of these objects can be dated accurately, but at least they show that the Indians who lived in Oregon when Crater Lake was formed were not unskilled in the primitive arts. Undoubtedly they were hunters, living on the banks of rivers, marshes, and lakes, and their principal diet was waterfowl and fish."

We asked, finally, if human skeletons or any other bones had yet been discovered in the pumice. "Yes," he replied, "two human skulls and the bones of several other individuals have been found in the pumice along the Medford highway between Prospect and McLeod. However, the remains lay in such a position that we are still in doubt whether the persons were actually killed by the glowing avalanches or were buried in the pumice long marked, "that except for the peak of Mount Mazama and the glaciers the landscape looked pretty much as it does now."

"Yes," said the Naturalist; "probably the only other important difference was that the forests on the higher slopes of the volcano were not so thick as they are today."

The young geologist asked if any information could be gained from a study of Wizard Island.

"The oldest trees on the island," replied the Naturalist, "are said to be about 900 years of age. Presumably, they began to grow soon after the last eruptions on the island. If so, the final volcanic activity within the park occurred less than 1000 years ago. This gives us a minimum age for Crater Lake. Unfortunately, we cannot tell how long it took for Wizard Island to grow."

"Isn't it possible to use the radiocarbon method of dating?" someone asked. "You've told us that there is a lot of charred wood within the deposits of the glowing avalanches. Has any of this been dated?"

"Yes," he replied. "Before Dr. Willard Libby discovered this method of dating, geologists could only use the rather vague evidence I've already discussed, and this led them to conclude that Mount Mazama collapsed between 5 and 10 thousand years ago. Now, radiocarbon dating of charcoal fragments within the glowing avalanche deposits and of material from archaeological sites buried by Mazama ash has shown that the climactic outburst of the volcano occurred approximately 6,600 years ago. The estimates by geologists were therefore very accurate."

told us that on the slopes of the Cascades farther north the pumice blown from Mount Mazama covers the youngest glacial moraines, and that very little soil has yet developed from it except in thick, damp woods. These facts also suggested that the great eruptions had happened rather recently.

"Several years ago," he continued, "when a trail was made along the rim of the lake between The Watchman and Discovery Point, the charred stump of a cedar tree was found inside the pumice, standing upright in the position of growth, with its uncharred roots embedded in the glacial moraine below. The tree must have been flourishing there at an elevation of 7000 feet just before the pumice eruptions began. Other charred trees were uncovered near Union Creek when the highway from Medford to Diamond Lake was made. Study of the charcoal shows that the glowing avalanches burned forests almost exactly like those now living there. Near Chemult, on the Dalles-California highway, charred pieces of lodgepole pine may be seen in the pumice close to the roots of living lodgepoles. Fortunately, the growth rings in all these charred fragments of wood are wonderfully preserved, and experts say that they indicate a climate just like the present one. We know also, from the distribution of the pumice around the shores of Klamath Lake and Klamath Marsh, that when the eruptions occurred those bodies of water cannot have been more than a few feet deeper than they are today."

"I gather from what you say," one of the group rethe glowing avalanches left their heavy loads on the slopes of the mountain, the rivers have only been able to cut narrow, steep-walled canyons through the pumice deposits, and this in spite of the fact that the pumice is easily removed. Besides, the rivers themselves flow swiftly, and each spring, when the snows are melting, they acquire new stores of energy. I feel sure, therefore, that no geologist would hesitate to say that narrow gorges like those of Annie, Sun, Sand, and Castle creeks may have been excavated within a few thousand years."

We asked if there was any way of telling how long it would take rain and snow to supply all the water in Crater Lake, and he answered that it would be impossible because there was no accurate information about past rain and snowfall, nor about the rate at which water seeped through the walls at various stages.

Then a young geologist in the group asked how long it would take for the long slides of loose rock to develop on the walls of the lake.

"Considering how steep the walls are and the character of the lavas and ashes," he replied, "they have suffered little from erosion. Anyone who has seen the havoc caused by a single summer storm will agree that a few thousand years would suffice to form most of the slides. And we must not forget that much of the slides may have been produced when the top of the mountain collapsed. Slides just as large were formed at the time Krakatoa collapsed."

Others sitting near us had overheard the discussion and now turned their chairs to join our circle. The Naturalist

Kerr valleys and the one which passed by the Lodge here and spread down Munson Valley. Even these ended about a mile beyond the rim. On the cool north slope of the volcano the ice had retreated to elevations of more than 7000 feet."

"How can you possibly tell?" someone asked.

"When you drove from the Lodge down to Government Headquarters," he answered, "you probably noticed that the road winds over bouldery glacial moraines. Search as you will, you cannot find any pumice on top of the moraines. In the upper parts of Sun and Kerr valleys there is only a light sprinkle of pumice on the moraines. Everywhere else around the rim of the lake, pumice is plentiful. The most reasonable explanation is that the areas free from pumice were still covered by ice when the great eruptions began, whereas the pumice-covered parts of the rim were bare. Hence, when the eruptions took place, practically all the glaciers on the volcano were less than 3 miles long. If the top of the mountain still existed, the glaciers would be almost as long today as they were then. Yet, 20,000 years ago, when the glaciers advanced farthest, they covered the volcano from head to foot, and one of them was 17 miles long. There is only one conclusion to draw."

"You mean that the cold climate of the Ice Age must have ended long before the pumice eruptions started?"

He nodded; and continued, "There is a second clue which indicates that the eruptions which led to the destruction of the mountain happened not long ago. Since

How Old Is Crater Lake?

IN THE EVENING we met our friendly guide again. Over dinner we had debated the problem of how long ago the top of Mount Mazama had disappeared; and, having failed to agree, we now asked his opinion.

"Have you noticed," he answered, "that if you ask a geologist when a certain event took place he is almost sure to reply that it occurred in the course of such and such a geological period, perhaps in Cretaceous, perhaps in Tertiary times? I could answer in the same way, and tell you that the top of the mountain disappeared in post-Pleistocene times, but you might think that I was trying to evade the question and hide under a cloak of jargon. What you probably want to know is how many years ago the collapse took place."

"Yes," we said. "Can't you tell us even approximately?"

"The reason the geologist hesitates to date events by years," he went on, "is because his yardstick was not made to measure small units of time such as the historian and archaeologist consider. When I spoke earlier about events happening 15 or 20 million years ago, I was less hesitant, but now you have me on dangerous ground."

He motioned us to draw up our chairs and, after a few moments, continued. "Just before the top of the volcano vanished," he said, "the only glaciers that stretched beyond the present rim of Crater Lake were those in Sun and had passed, most of the island of Krakatoa had disappeared and a submarine caldera several miles wide had taken its place. Some who described the catastrophe thought that the volcano had 'blown its head off,' but we now know that the island was engulfed. Of all the material blown out, less than a tenth consists of shattered pieces of the former volcano. By far the most of it consists of pumice similar to that around Crater Lake. And there, as here, it was mainly the eruption of pumice from the underlying reservoir that caused collapse, and this in turn propelled the destructive tidal waves. Not only was a circular caldera formed, but the sea floor beyond caved in to produce two deep troughs. In 1927, after 44 years of rest, eruptions were renewed from an opening within the caldera. These have continued at intervals ever since and have built a cone of black cinders above the sea, just as Wizard Island was built on the floor of Crater Lake."

As he was about to leave, he turned and said, "Crater Lake, large as it is, is by no means the largest caldera in the world. There are several in Japan that are larger, and it may interest you to know that perhaps the largest of all lies among the Valles Mountains, not far from Santa Fe, New Mexico. Its dimensions are 15 by 18 miles. But though many calderas exceed Crater Lake in size, few—if, indeed, any—can rival it in majesty and none more clearly reveals the manner of its origin. Among the ruins of a giant volcano, Nature has here produced a lake of extraordinary beauty, and amid these inspiring surroundings has given us an opportunity to study her method of creation."

Mount Mazama Just Before the Destruction of Its Summit

—*From a painting by Paul Rockwood*

CRATER LAKE

THE STORY OF ITS ORIGIN

➤➤➤➤➤➤➤➤➤➤➤➤➤➤➤➤ ◄◄◄◄◄◄◄◄◄◄◄◄◄◄◄◄

BY HOWEL WILLIAMS

PROFESSOR OF GEOLOGY IN THE UNIVERSITY OF CALIFORNIA

UNIVERSITY OF CALIFORNIA PRESS

Berkeley, Los Angeles, London   1972

UNIVERSITY OF CALIFORNIA PRESS
BERKELEY AND LOS ANGELES, CALIFORNIA

UNIVERSITY OF CALIFORNIA PRESS, LTD.
LONDON, ENGLAND

MANUFACTURED IN THE UNITED STATES OF AMERICA

Preface

OUR NATIONAL PARKS *include some of the most majestic scenery in the world. They are visited every year by hundreds of thousands in search of relaxation and enjoyment, and, thanks to the efforts of the Naturalist Staff of the Park Service, the educational values of the parks are gaining rapidly in appeal. To the geologist the parks present a special opportunity to be of public service; by interpreting the origin of landscapes and revealing the age-long operation of natural forces involved in their growth, it becomes his privilege to offer the visitor a possibility of appreciating more fully the scenery of our parks.*

There are many to whom the visual beauty of Crater Lake is enough in itself. This book has been written in the hope that some may find added pleasure when their imaginations are stirred by thoughts of how the beauty came into being. It tries to describe how, through millions of years, the present landscape was sculptured. In nontechnical language it seeks to conjure up pictures of former scenes the existence of which made the present beauty possible.

The book is divided into two parts. In the first I have attempted to describe the changing scenes of the past as a privileged eyewitness might have done. In the second I have sought to present some of the evidence in the form of a discussion between a guide and a group of question-

ing visitors, my purpose being to sustain the interest of
the layman not versed in the methods and language of
the geologist.

The visitor trained in geology needs no guidance other
than that supplied by the maps and sections which are
included with the text. Using these, he may seek the evidence for himself. To others suggestions are offered concerning the best places to visit, and it is hoped that by
following the discussion they may begin to see how the
geologist goes about his task of reconstructing the story
of the past.

The work upon which the book is based was begun four
years ago under the auspices of the National Academy
of Sciences. To Dr. John C. Merriam, chairman of the
Academy's Committee on Scientific Problems in the National Parks, I owe a special debt of gratitude, not only
for generous funds which he placed at my disposal, but
also for his personal interest and kindly encouragement.
To the Board of Research of the University of California
I acknowledge my indebtedness for additional funds.

The officials of the National Park Service at Crater
Lake facilitated the work by many courtesies. More particularly, I should like to acknowledge the kindness of
the former and present Superintendents, Mr. David Can-
field and Mr. E. P. Leavitt, respectively, Mr. John E. Doerr,
Jr., former Park Naturalist, and his assistants, Mr. Wayne
E. Kartchner and Mr. Loren Miller. It gives me pleasure
also to thank Mr. Randall Brown and Mr. Roy Turner,
each of whom assisted me in the field for a season.

Members of the staff of the Western Museum Laboratories of the National Park Service, at Emeryville, California, have aided in many ways. During the preparation of the manuscript, Mr. George Watson and Mr. Lawrence Moffett gave much valuable advice, based on their long experience in the popular presentation of geological matters. Mr. Paul Rockwood's splendid contribution speaks for itself in the excellent paintings reproduced in Plates I, II a, and IV. Mr. A. W. Severy kindly prepared the maps.

For the use of photographs I am grateful to the United States Army Air Corps, the Washington National Guard, the National Park Service, and Mr. Wm. Schoeb. For information concerning the former forests of Oregon I am indebted to Dr. R. W. Chaney, and for permission to quote verses from his book of poems, Blue Interval, *I am indebted to Professor E. G. Moll. The information concerning early man in the Crater Lake region is based on the work of Professor L. S. Cressman.*

HOWEL WILLIAMS

Department of Geological Sciences,
University of California,
Berkeley, California.

Contents

Illustrations

PLATES

Figures in Text

INTRODUCTION

Introduction

There rolls the deep where grew the tree,
O earth, what changes thou hast seen!
There where the long street roars, hath been
The stillness of the central sea.

TENNYSON, *In Memoriam*

HILLS AND VALLEYS, mountains and canyons, waterfalls and meadows bring delight to the eye, but only if they are endowed with some extraordinary quality of form or color do they rouse questions about their origin. Landscapes are usually taken for granted, as if they had existed unchanged since time began, once sculptured by mysterious forces and thereafter left untouched. To understand the geologic history of any region, we must before all else abandon completely the illusion that what we see is permanent. Far from being everlasting, the scenes with which we are familiar are ever-changing. Our lifetimes are so short compared with the enormous spans of geologic time that we are apt to minimize the slight changes that take place incessantly on hill and valley alike. In the course of a severe storm, landslides leave new scars, and fresh gullies are cut by powerful torrents. On the coast, heavy waves batter the cliffs; in the mountains, the roar of avalanches at the time of melting snow tells of havoc being wrought. Winds move sand dunes in the desert, and rivers in flood widen their banks, carrying loads of debris to the sea.

[3]

Taken singly, these seem trivial incidents. Yet in countless ways, many of them scarcely perceptible, the relentless attack of frost, ice, snow, rain, wind, and waves remodels the landscape before our eyes.

Perhaps geology has no more significant lesson to teach than this: all landscapes are evanescent. Nor is the change confined to the land. In rocks now far from the sea, even on the summits of mountains, are embedded the remains of marine organisms. The rocks in which these fossils lie must once have been sands and muds on the ocean floor, and in ages to come they will wear away to become sands and muds again, and be carried back by rivers to the ocean bed. New forms of life will be buried; the sediments will be hardened again into rocks; and finally, after millions of years, the rocks will be crumpled, fractured, and upheaved to form new mountains. The cycle, no sooner than complete, begins anew. The sea is at once the grave and the birthplace of the land. "Nothing," wrote Darwin, "not even the wind that blows, is so unstable as the level crust of this earth."

The climate also changes. Some desert countries were formerly clothed with dense tropical forests, and the green slopes around Crater Lake were once covered by thick sheets of ice. And as the distribution of land and sea and the nature of the climate change, so do the forms of life. All is change.

Long before the traveler reaches Crater Lake, he finds himself surrounded by volcanic rocks. Inside the park, he begins to climb the slopes of an ancient volcano. With breathtaking suddenness he reaches the brink of a tremendous caldron, between 5 and 6 miles wide, enclosing a lake of surpassing beauty. Even the seasoned traveler, surfeited with scenery, gasps in astonishment; even the habitual visitor thrills each time he comes to the rim. Twenty miles of cliffs, tinted in delicate shades of red and brown and yellow, and fringed with the rich greens of hemlock, pine, and fir, cast their reflections in a mirror of indescribable blue.

> These beauteous forms,
> Through a long absence, have not been to me
> As is a landscape to a blind man's eye:
> But oft, in lonely rooms and 'mid the din
> Of towns and cities, I have owed to them
> In hours of weariness, sensations sweet,
> Felt in the blood, and felt along the heart;
> And passing even into my purer mind,
> With tranquil restoration.
>
> WORDSWORTH, *Tintern Abbey*

No thoughtful visitor can stand for long on the edge of this stupendous caldron without wondering how it was formed. How did a lake of such rare beauty come to occupy the top of an old volcano? The gentle slopes outside the rim resemble the lower slopes of other volcanoes, like Shasta, Rainier, and Hood. A giant peak must therefore have towered above the lake. Others have named this vanished peak Mount Mazama. In this book is told the story of the growth and destruction, the rise and fall of this ancient mountain, and consequently the origin of Crater Lake itself.

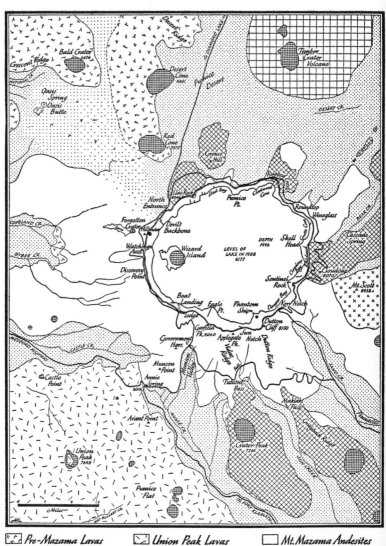

Geologic map of Crater Lake National Park.

PART ONE: THE STORY

Before Mount Mazama Was

The hills are shadows, and they flow
From form to form, and nothing stands;
They melt like mist, the solid lands,
Like clouds they shape themselves and go.

TENNYSON, *In Memoriam*

MORE THAN 60 million years ago, in what geologists call the late Cretaceous period, a wide and shallow sea rolled over what is now the Cascade Range. At that time the Coast Ranges of Oregon and California were submerged and the waves of the Pacific lapped against the foothills of the Sierra Nevada and the Blue Mountains of eastern Oregon. Where the Cascade peaks now rise in lofty grandeur, water teemed with shellfish—long since become extinct. Giant marine lizards swam in the seas, and winged reptiles sailed above in search of prey. On the neighboring coasts grotesque dinosaurs lived among tropical vegetation.

Toward the close of the Cretaceous period the entire western part of this continent was subjected to profound earth movements. The rocks of the crust were folded and fractured, not by a cataclysmic process, but gradually during millions of years, just as our coastal ranges are being disturbed today. As a result of these movements the seas were driven westward beyond the present line of the Cascade Range, never to return. At the same time, the bending and breaking of the rocks relieved pressure on the hot

[9]

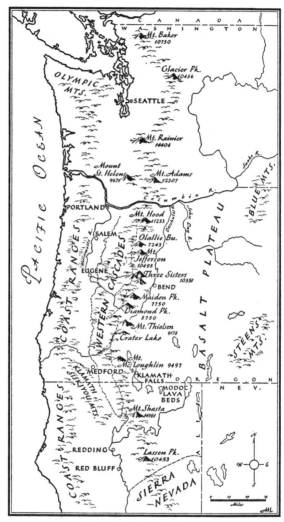

Map of the Cascade Range.

material beneath the earth's crust and permitted lava to rise to the surface through cracks from the deep interior. From Washington southward along the Cascades and the Sierra Nevada, volcanoes burst into activity.

During the succeeding Eocene and Oligocene epochs, between about 60 and 25 million years ago, the region around Crater Lake was a low, rolling plain crossed by broad, winding rivers. Far to the east, over what is now the John Day Basin, there were large fresh-water lakes. Rising above the plain were scores of dark volcanoes, some surrounded by barren sheets of rugged lava and others by sterile piles of newly fallen ash. Along the coast, near Roseburg, low volcanic islands rose from the sea. The Klamath Mountains were then very much lower than they are today, and along their eastern edge, in the present Ashland-Medford valley, there were dense swamps where peat accumulated from rotted vegetation, to be converted later into coal. From time to time the forests were destroyed by showers of hot ash or drowned by swollen rivers dammed by flows of lava. The vegetation was remarkably different from that of today. It was like that on the lower slopes of the Andes in Venezuela, on the savannas of Panama, and in the mountains of Costa Rica and Guatemala. Avocados, cinnamons, figs, and persimmons flourished. On the volcanic hills above the plains the tropical vegetation was mixed with trees of temperate species, including the redwood, alder, tan oak, and elm. Small, graceful horses, not more than a foot high, roamed the open spaces.

Throughout Eocene and Oligocene times and on to the close of the Miocene epoch, approximately 11 or 12 million years ago, volcanoes continued to erupt. Their lavas and ashes were piled on each other until in places their thickness approached 10,000 feet. By the close of the Miocene epoch the low plains of Eocene days had been changed into a plateau of moderate elevation. Extensive lakes still occupied much of central Oregon, for there was no Cascade Range to check the moisture-laden winds from blowing far inland. Redwoods grew in the John Day country, together with black and live oaks, box elders, madroños, plane trees, and poplars. Near the coast, in sheltered valleys, some of the tropical and subtropical vegetation still survived. Rhinoceroses and small camels, giant hogs as large as full-grown bulls, peccaries, tapirs, delicate-limbed antelopes, and little horses five or six hands tall, wandered through the woods, while wolves and huge, saber-toothed cats preyed on the weaker beasts. Drowned by floods and killed by ash, their bones have been preserved for us in the wonderful fossil beds of the John Day country.

While the Miocene volcanoes were active in western Oregon, eruptions of a different kind were taking place on an unprecedented scale in eastern Oregon and eastern Washington. Throughout this vast area the earth's crust was broken by innumerable cracks, from which were erupted floods of highly liquid lava. Time and again the molten material gushed to the surface. Instead of piling around the cracks to form volcanic cones, the lava spread in wide sheets over the older landscape, transforming more than 200,000 square miles of country into barren, black plains. It would be difficult to picture a more desolate scene.

Throughout this long period of volcanic activity the earth's crust was repeatedly bent and broken. At the end of Miocene times the disturbances reached a climax. It was then that the Cascade Range first took shape as a distinct mountain belt, by upheaval and bending of the thick blanket of volcanic rocks laid down during the earlier epochs. It was then, for the first time, that moisture-laden winds from the sea were prevented by a high barrier from reaching eastern Oregon. Redwoods continued to grow on the wet western slopes, but to the east of the range they disappeared and a desert vegetation not unlike the present one took their place.

When the Cascade Range was upheaved, many north–south fractures were opened along and near the crest, and in the course of the next 10 million years, throughout the Pliocene epoch, the lavas that poured from these fractures built a series of new volcanic cones. One of these, the Union Peak volcano, rose to the southwest of Crater Lake; another, Mount Thielsen, grew farther to the north. Unlike the earlier ones, these Pliocene volcanoes were seldom violent, but erupted their lavas quietly, as the volcanoes of Hawaii do today.

During Pliocene times, the forests of Oregon were not essentially different from those of the present. The animals, though beginning to look more like modern types, still included many strange forms. There were long-

SEQUENCE OF EVENTS IN THE CRATER LAKE REGION

Period	Epoch	Nature of events	Approximate duration in years
Quaternary	Recent	Postglacial time. Concluding activity and destruction of Mount Mazama. Formation of Crater Lake. Man appears in the region.	10,000–20,000
	Pleistocene	The Great Ice Age. The main period of growth of Mounts Mazama, Hood, Shasta, and Rainier.	1–2 million
Tertiary	Pliocene	Building of pre-Mazama volcanoes of the High Cascades, e.g. Union Peak. Climate becoming cooler. Modern forests.	10 million
	Miocene and Oligocene	Widespread volcanic activity over most of Oregon. Tremendous eruptions of lava from fissures in eastern part of state during Middle Miocene times. Upheaval of Cascade Range at close of epoch. Climate becoming cooler. Redwood forests predominant.	25 million
	Eocene	Earth movements drive out the seas and volcanic activity begins at the opening of the epoch. Tropical forests cover the plains, and temperate forests the hills.	25 million
Cretaceous	Cretaceous	Wide, shallow, tropical seas cover most of Oregon during the later portion of the epoch. No volcanic activity.	75 million

limbed, long-necked giraffe-camels, and bear-dogs as large as the largest Alaska brown bears. Short-legged, semi-aquatic rhinoceroses lived along the streams and on the edge of marshes. The horses, though hardly bigger than ponies, were larger than they had been in earlier days.

Meanwhile the climate had been growing steadily colder. Snows falling on the high peaks no longer melted in the summer sun, but lingered through the year. As the snow fields piled deeper, they developed into glaciers. All over the northern part of the continent, not only in the mountainous western parts, but even over the low country to the east, ice sheets of enormous proportions began to form. The world was about to undergo another and the last of its great Ice Ages. It was under these conditions that Mount Mazama was formed.

How Mount Mazama Rose

Out of the ancient rage of fire and frost
And prisoned forces struggling to be free
Came beauty such as poets, vision-lost,
Dreamed long ago in dales of Arcady.

MOLL, *Blue Interval*

BETWEEN 1 and 2 millions of years ago, a crack opened in the earth's crust a short distance south of what was later to become the middle of Crater Lake. This event heralded the birth of a new volcano.

Far beneath the surface the rocks were intensely hot. Forty miles down they were so hot that they would have been completely molten had it not been for the enormous weight which pressed upon them and held them solid. When the earth's crust cracked, the pressure on the deep-seated rocks was suddenly relieved and they began at once to melt. Gradually they changed to a red-hot, pasty substance, magma, and this slowly made its way upward from the depths. When the magma had risen to within 3 to 5 miles of the surface, it began to spread sideways, squeezing the adjacent rocks apart, and so came to occupy a large chamber. This was the reservoir of molten rock that was later to supply the lavas and ashes which built Mount Mazama.

For a time the pasty magma was imprisoned by the rocky walls of the chamber. But it held within itself the means of escape, for it was richly charged with gas. At first the gas was dissolved in the liquid, like the gas in a firmly corked bottle of champagne, and it was held in that condition as long as the confining pressure remained. When new cracks opened in the roof of the magma chamber the effect was the same as that which takes place when the cork is removed from the bottle of champagne. Great quantities of gas separated from the liquid in the form of bubbles, and just as the foaming champagne rushes up the neck of the bottle and overflows, so the bubbling, effervescing magma forced its way outward to the surface. The growth of Mount Mazama had begun.

Just before the first outburst, curling wisps of vapor could be seen rising from the cracks. Shortly thereafter the discharge of vapor suddenly increased. There were loud roars and the ground in the vicinity shook violently. Fragments of rock were torn from the sides of the cracks by uprushing gases and were hurled into the air. The volcano was "clearing its throat"; it was opening vents or outlets for itself. Soon the activity became more spectacular, for the fragments blown out were no longer dark. At night, many were white-hot as they rose from the vents; others were a golden color, and even the coolest glowed with a cherry-red light. These were not solid lumps of old rock, but incandescent clots of new magma blown from the underlying chamber. Though they cooled in their flight through the air, most of them were still semimolten when they struck the ground. When they had thoroughly cooled they bore a curious resemblance to cindery lumps in a fire grate. As the eruptions continued, the fragments accumulated around the vents in the form of a cone, and the vents themselves developed into steep-walled funnels. At times the violent explosive eruptions died down and lava surged out through the funnel-shaped craters and spilled over the rims in floods. There were days when the lava was so hot and fluid that it rushed down the sides of the cone with the speed of a mountain brook. Its temperature then was not less than 1800° Fahrenheit. On other days the lava was much cooler and contained much less gas, so that it crawled down the sides of the cone with the sluggish motion of thick tar. Sometimes the flows had a twisted, ropelike crust, and at other times they were broken into angular blocks so that they resembled beds of smoldering coals. Flow piled on flow, adding continually to the height and width of the cone. After several months the activity subsided and the magma in the feeding pipes slowly congealed, forming rigid plugs. The volcano had entered into a stage of inactivity.

But while all was quiet at the surface, changes were taking place in the underground reservoir, preparing the way for a new outburst. The magma was cooling against the rocky sides of the chamber. In so doing, part of it began to solidify, and the concentration of gas in the remaining liquid steadily increased until bubbles again began to form. Slowly these rose through the liquid toward the top of the chamber, and eventually the pressure of the gases became so great that they blasted a channel to the surface. A new phase of eruption was started. The rigid plugs of

—*From a painting by Paul Rockwood*

MOUNT MAZAMA AT THE TIME OF MAXIMUM GLACIATION

—*Photo National Park Service*

ICE SCRATCHES AND POLISH ON THE RIM NEAR DISCOVERY POINT

—Photo A. Lacroix
A GLOWING AVALANCHE FROM MONT PELÉ (WEST INDIES) IN 1902

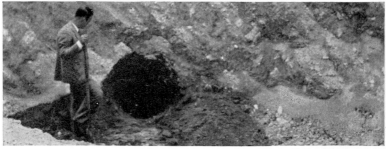

—Photo National Park Service
CHARCOAL LOG IN PUMICE LEFT BY A GLOWING AVALANCHE, DIAMOND LAKE
HIGHWAY, NEAR UNION CREEK JUNCTION

solid lava which had temporarily sealed the pipes were blown out and once more magma foamed into the craters. Again, violent explosions alternated with quiet outpouring of lava. Layer after layer of material was added to the surface of the growing volcano. For hundreds of thousands of years, periods of quiet, often lasting for centuries, inter-

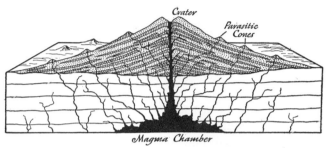

Ideal section across a composite volcanic cone. Ashes and other fragmental layers are shown by dots, lava flows by line pattern. Both cone and basement are cut by swarms of dikes.

rupted the periods of activity. And in every outburst it was the gas in the magma that was the driving force. In large measure it was the amount and pressure of the gas which determined whether the magma was poured out as lava or blown out in the form of ash and light, frothy pumice. When the gas content was high, the lava sometimes spouted hundreds of feet into the air in fiery fountains and cascaded swiftly down the mountainsides; when there was little gas, the flows were so pasty that they were only able to creep a few hundred yards downhill. By far the greater part of the gas was water vapor, and it was this, mainly, that formed the gigantic cauliflower-shaped clouds which so commonly rose from the craters. With the water vapor there was usually much carbon dioxide, carbon monoxide, various sulphur compounds, and a relatively small proportion of hydrofluoric and hydrochloric acid gas. Some idea of the enormous amount of gas discharged may be gained when we recall that long after the pumice was laid down in the Valley of Ten Thousand Smokes, Alaska, in 1912, the deposits continued to emit 6 million gallons of steam per second, and each year they delivered into the atmosphere 1,250,000 tons of hydrochloric acid and 200,000 tons of hydrofluoric acid.

After Mount Mazama had risen to a height of several thousand feet, eruptions took place more and more from openings on the flanks instead of from the summit. It became increasingly difficult and often impossible for the lava to overflow from the tops of the central pipes, for the pipes were clogged to a great depth with already solidified material. When they were thoroughly sealed in this fashion the upward pressure of the magma was often powerful enough to crack the entire cone. Some of the cracks branched from the central pipes; others tapped the reservoir still farther down. No sooner were the cracks opened than they were filled with molten rock. Occasionally the cracks were wedged open to the surface, so that torrents of incandescent lava burst from the sides of the volcano and swept down the slopes. At night the flows seemed like rivers of fire and the clouds of vapor that rose above them were lit by a lurid glow. So much vapor was

discharged by these streams of lava that when they cooled
and hardened they were crowded with blisters and empty
bubbles; in places the rocks looked like solidified froth.
Occasionally, again, the magma escaped from the cracks
more violently, in showers of fragments. The outrushing
gases roared thunderously, and the surging clouds of
steam were shot through with scintillating flashes of lightning.

On the slopes of the growing mountain were boiling
pools and geysers, and wisps of hot gas rose quietly from
a thousand fissures. Near these places the dark, drab lavas
were decomposed and their colors were changed to pink,
yellow, brown, and green. Where they were thoroughly
altered by the hot solutions the rocks were changed to
beautifully tinted muds that spattered continually like
boiling porridge.

After more than a million years, Mount Mazama had
risen to a height of almost 12,000 feet, towering far above
its neighbors. In the whole length of the Cascade Range
there were few volcanoes that rivaled it in size. Now the
eruptions from the summit virtually ceased. A semicircular crack opened halfway down the northern slope. Here
and there, thick flows of lava rose slowly from the crack
and crept downward in jagged tongues. At other points
along the crack, explosions of terrifying strength blasted
deep craters through the mountainside. Shortly thereafter,
lava welled sluggishly into the craters and buried them
under giant mounds, one of them more than 1000 feet
high. The crust of the pasty lava was chilled to jet-black

glass, and as this was borne along by the slow spread of the molten material below, it was shattered into ragged pinnacles. Blocks of glass tumbled continually from the fronts and sides of the creeping flows with a tinkling sound like the noise of breaking crockery, and wherever blocks broke loose, the liquid lava inside was revealed, glowing bright red until it, in turn, was chilled to glass.

Meanwhile, more than a score of other vents were blasted open farther down the mountain and even on the flats to the east. From these, red-hot clots of magma were hurled in showers. Some of the clots were more than a yard across, but most were not larger than peas and walnuts. The larger lumps were hotter and at night they shone with a more brilliant light, and as they spun through the air they were molded into globular and ropy forms. Some were so hot that even after describing fiery arcs in the air they splashed when they struck the ground, but most of them fell to earth with a rattling noise. When they were cool they looked like clinkers. Now one vent offered its pyrotechnic display; then its fury died down, and another began. In time a large cone of fragments was built around each vent. Occasionally, streams of foaming lava oozed through the sides of the cones; on other days, columns of steam rose lazily from their summits.

After many years the eruptions waned and ended. Once more, verdure spread over the ash-covered landscape. For centuries the mountain slumbered. The lower slopes were green with trees and meadows. But the peace outside merely concealed the changes that were going on within.

Glaciers of Mount Mazama

THROUGHOUT the Tertiary period in North America the climate had been growing cooler and the warmth-loving vegetation had been migrating southward. Finally, a million or at most two million years ago, about the time that Mount Mazama first erupted, the climate became so cold that almost the whole of Canada and most of our northern states were covered by an enormously thick blanket of ice, like those which still cover Greenland and Antarctica. Local ice fields developed along the crest of the Cascade Range and the Sierra Nevada and spread for miles down the valleys on either side.

Long before Mount Mazama had grown to its maximum size, even when it was still only a few thousand feet high, flaky snow began to pile around the summit, for the heat of summer was no longer sufficient to remove the snow which fell in winter. As the snow piled deeper, it gradually packed under its own weight and changed to granular ice, and when this gained mass enough, it began, at an almost imperceptible rate, to move down the sides

of the volcano. Thin tongues of ice or glaciers crept downward into the valleys previously carved by rivers. As they
did so, they gathered an ever-increasing load of shattered
rock. Part of the load they picked up from the rocky walls
of the valleys, for with every frost and rain, fragments
were loosened and fell to the glaciers from the neighboring cliffs. Many of the fragments found their way down
cracks in the ice and became firmly embedded in the interior; the rest accumulated on the margins in the form of
long embankments or lateral moraines. Still other rock
waste was picked up by the glaciers from the valley floors.
Before the tongues of ice had traveled far, they were
heavily laden with angular boulders, pebbles, sand, and
finely pulverized rock powder. Where the glaciers were
a thousand feet thick, the weight on the floor was not less
than 28 tons on each square foot. Under the enormous
load, the stones frozen into the base of the ice scoured the
valley floors. While the larger fragments gouged deep
grooves, the rock powder polished the surface until it
fairly glistened like a finely scratched mirror. Even today,
thousands of years later, polished slabs of rock remain to
tell of the passage of the glaciers. (See plate facing p. 18.)

However, the ice exerted a much more profound in-
fluence on the landscape than the mere polishing and
scratching of the rocks over which it moved. The valleys
which the early rivers had cut on the sides of the volcano
were like those which other rivers are cutting today in
mountainous regions. They were winding, and their slopes
descended to the floor like the sides of a letter V. When

the glaciers spread down these valleys, they ground away the projecting spurs and undercut the sides. For thousands of years the icy fingers scratched and sculptured. When the climate became warmer and the snowfall decreased, the glaciers shrank and retreated up the mountainsides. The valleys they left behind were no longer winding, but

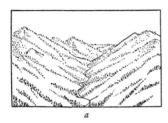 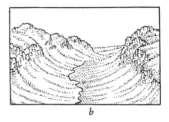

Valley forms. *a*. V-shaped, river-cut valley. *b*. The same valley changed by glacial action into a U-shaped canyon.

straight; the sides were steeper, and the floors were wider and flatter, so that in cross section the valleys were U-shaped. On the valley floors the melting ice left rocky refuse piles in its wake. The debris which had fallen on the margins of the glaciers from the adjacent walls was left stranded in long ridges close to the valley sides, and the debris which had been frozen within the ice was left in hummocky mounds all over the valley floors. Roaring torrents of water poured from the melting ice and spread over the flats around the mountain's base. From time to time, flows of lava and showers of red-hot ash destroyed some of the glaciers completely and the raging melt-waters swept the valley bottoms clean. When the glaciers vanished, forests spread up the valleys after them. The stony places were clothed in green once more. Lodgepole pines, then whitebark, sugar, and yellow pines, cedars, hemlocks, and firs advanced in files along the sun-bathed moraines. In spring and summer, carpets of gaily colored flowers made the open spaces bright. After a long interval, even the black and jagged beds of lava, which had formerly seemed so stark, were covered with grass. The hum of insects and the song of birds filled the air. The silent wastes of ice were transformed into a scene of joyful peace.

But the strife was far from ended. Eruptions continued and the summit of the mountain steadily increased in height as lava piled on lava. Now more snow than ever fell from the passing clouds. Fed by the heavier snowfall, the glaciers crept back into the valleys with renewed strength, spreading far beyond their former limits. Bearing down on their rocky beds, they resumed their grinding, gouging, and polishing. Soon all but the very crests of the ridges were covered with a white mantle. When the volcano burst into activity, fiery streams of lava broke through the ice and columns of ash rose from the craters. The clouds over the summit reflected the fitful, red glare of the lava on the dazzling ice, so that the whole mountain glowed with a pinkish light.

Finally, the ice made its last and greatest advance. It choked even the deepest canyons and overflowed the divides. The largest glaciers moved down the western slope of the volcano and united into a single body of ice in the valley of the Rogue. The front of this main glacier lay not less than 17 miles from the summit of the mountain. On the north side of the volcano the glaciers were so thick that they covered all but the top of Desert Ridge. Spreading beyond, they coalesced with glaciers from Mounts Bailey and Thielsen and made an expansive field of ice over what is now Diamond Lake. On the east slope of the volcano the glaciers moved downward to the plateau now crossed by the Dalles-California highway, and large rivers poured from them carrying heavy loads of sand and gravel into the Klamath Marsh, which was then much deeper than it is today. On the south side of the volcano one glacier passed by the present site of Crater Lake Lodge and the adjacent Camp Grounds and so made its way into the canyon of Annie Creek. Another poured through Sun Notch, and a third through Kerr Notch. For a time these three glaciers were so thick that they spread across the intervening ridges and united in an unbroken sheet. The whole of the Union Peak volcano was also covered with ice.

About 20,000 years ago the snowfall diminished and the summer heat melted the glaciers faster than they were replenished from above. The ice fronts began to make their last retreat. First the glaciers abandoned the ridges; then they withdrew up the canyons, leaving their burden of rock waste behind. When their length had been reduced to 3 or 4 miles, a new phase in the volcanic history of Mount Mazama began.

The Climax of Destruction

Now a cloud of smoke,
Whirlwinds of pitch, and embers glowing white,
To the frayed stars he flings, and globes of fire.
Now shattered stones and entrails of the mount
He belches forth, and volleys molten rocks,
Roaring, and boiling from his deep abyss.

VERGIL, *Aeneid* (Billson trans.)

THE STAGE was now set; the fateful eruptions that led to the disappearance of the top of the mountain were about to begin. How the volcano looked at this critical time may be seen in the painting reproduced as the frontispiece to this book. The glaciers that had once covered the mountain to its foot were confined to the summit region. Only on the south side did they extend lower than the present rim of Crater Lake, and even here they were but small relics. Ice still covered the area now occupied by Crater Lake Lodge and the Camp Grounds and continued down Munson Valley as far as Government Headquarters, and thin tongues of ice still passed through Sun and Kerr notches, ending a mile below. None of the other glaciers on the mountain was more than 3 miles long. The upper slopes of the mountain were almost barren. Here and there, clumps of trees grew along what is now the crater rim, but the thick forests were much farther down, beyond the boundaries of the present Park.

[28]

A long period of quiet preceded the culminating eruptions. All that time, the pressure of the gases in the underground chamber was gradually increasing. Finally, the roof of the chamber was no longer able to withstand it, and the volcano entered upon the most explosive phase of its long history.

The opening day was clear and the morning light shone brilliantly on the ice around the summit. Suddenly there was an ominous rumbling underground, and a moment later a plume of steam rose from the crater. The slumbering volcano had awakened. Within a few minutes the plume over the summit assumed a globular form and then, with alarming speed, expanded into a giant cloud shaped like a cauliflower. The billowy mass rose miles into the upper air, and there the wind drew it out into fleecy banks that drifted to the east. The rumbling noises grew louder and peals of thunder echoed over the mountain, interspersed with sharper detonations like the discharge of heavy guns. Frenzied flashes of lightning zigzagged through the cloud. Soon the sun was obscured and in the failing light showers of ash could be seen dropping like a rain of liquid fire. Close to the mountain, the larger fragments were white-hot in their upward flight, and as they turned and fell they changed first to a golden color and then to orange, and many were red before they struck the ground. Farther away, the falling fragments were cooler and their color was leaden gray. At night the eruption cloud was lit from below by the glow of lava in the crater and from within by myriads of incandescent sparks. Thun derous roars interrupted the staccato snapping of lightning. The hot ash had begun to melt the surface of the glaciers, and when the noise of thunder subsided, the sound of swollen torrents could be heard above the dull patter of falling stones. Frightened birds screeched, and the loud clamor of terrified beasts filled the woods.

Day after day, night after night, the eruptions continued. There were brief intervals of comparative calm, but each was brought to a close by an outburst more violent than the one preceding. It was now increasingly difficult to see what was happening on the mountain. Fine dust and the smoke of forest fires permeated the air. The hot, acid fumes were suffocating. As the activity grew in strength, the winds veered toward the northeast, in the direction of what is now the town of Bend. The falling fragments, which at first had scarcely been larger than peas, were now as large as a man's fist. Over thousands of square miles the air was so charged with dust that the days were darker than the blackest night. Close to the mountain, it was impossible to see one's outstretched hand. Far off, on the plateau to the east, small bands of Indians gathered in dumb horror about their campfires, too bewildered to flee for safety. They had often seen the mountain burst into flame before, but this cataclysm, this ashy darkness, seemed to be the end of everything.

After several weeks, these preliminary eruptions—for such they turned out to be—died down, the atmosphere cleared, and a desolate scene met the eye. The landscape had a wintry aspect, for the freshly fallen pumice looked uncannily like snow. Over everything lay a gray-white pall. Even to the south and west of the mountain, where the destruction was least, the trees were no longer green, but were covered with impalpable dust like flour. In the opposite direction the mantle of whitish pumice stretched for hundreds of miles. Near the base of the mountain were places where the pumice banks were 20 feet thick, and even 70 miles away the sheet of fragments was a foot thick. Far beyond, over Washington and much of Canada, a coating of fine dust covered everything. In the evenings the western sky was filled with amazing lights. The setting sun changed from pale green through gold to deep blood red. The vast, dust-charged clouds were never the same color for more than a moment. One instant, they seemed like shining brass and tarnished copper; the next, they were streaked with brick red, lemon, and orange. As the last rays shone, the whole sky was aflame. A display no less astounding accompanied every sunrise.

Fearsome as the first weeks of activity had been, they were only a prelude to the more violent eruptions that followed. The climax came with startling rapidity. There were no loud explosions to herald its approach. At first, a puff of steam rose from the summit of the mountain. Quickly it developed into an enormous cloud like a cluster of rapidly expanding balloons. It was composed of countless seething convolutions and was illuminated from below with a ruddy glare. Suddenly there was an ear-splitting roar; the cloud spread like a mushroom and settled over the summit in billowing folds. It rolled and surged down the mountainsides with ever-increasing speed. A few miles below the summit a strange thing happened: the cloud divided into many branches that poured into the canyons like raging torrents. At the base of each advancing cloud there was an incandescent avalanche of fragments. Close to the ground the avalanches were brilliantly luminous. Upward, they changed to gold and deeper reds. The clouds of vapor which half concealed the glowing base were dense gray and brown in their lower parts, but higher up, where they contained less ash, they were lighter gray, and at the top they were snowy white. Sheets and forks of lightning darted in all directions. The velocity of the onrushing avalanches was staggering. Many swept along at more than a hundred miles an hour. Yet the sides and fronts of the overhanging clouds rose almost vertically for thousands of feet, boiling with incredible energy. No less amazing was the quietness of the fiery avalanches as they raced along the canyons. Instead of a deafening roar, there was a sound as of wind among treetops.

When the glowing avalanches entered the forests near the base of the mountain, the crackling of burning trees could be heard, and soon the sides of the canyons were marked by avenues of flame. Racing onward, the avalanches compressed the air in advance until it was scorching hot, and the violent winds mowed down the trees like skittles. Large trunks were snapped off by the gales.

It was astonishing how far the avalanches rushed. Those that swept down the canyons on the western slopes of the mountain entered the valley of the Rogue and only came to an end near the present village of McLeod, a distance of more than 35 miles from the source, despite the fact that during the second half of their journey they crashed through heavy timber. Those that poured northward swept over the surface of Diamond Lake and emptied into the valley of the North Umpqua. Those that raced toward the northeast circled round the base of Timber Crater and spread out on the plateau beyond, and such was their momentum that they plunged over the flat ground for a distance of 25 miles from the summit of the mountain. Other glowing avalanches crashed down Scott and Bear creeks and deployed into the Klamath Marsh, and from there great masses of floating pumice were washed down the Williamson River into the Klamath Lakes. Still other avalanches poured down Sun, Sand, and Annie creeks.

What was it that gave the avalanches such prodigious strength, such astounding mobility? In part it was the momentum of the heavy loads as they tumbled headlong down the steep, upper slopes of the volcano. But, more important, it was the high content of hot gas. These avalanches were literally flows of incandescent magma and dense, violently expanding gas, a kind of glowing emulsion composed of pasty lumps and droplets discharging gas at extremely high temperatures and pressures. The turbulent mixture was mobile because each particle was cushioned by gas. As each semisolid fragment burst open, explosions urged the mass onward with hurricane speed. It was the presence of all this expanding gas which accounted for the eery quietness of the avalanches and for their power to wipe out all obstacles in their path. Instead of sliding over the ground, they were buoyed up so that they rolled and sprang along in bounds. No wonder that enormous lumps were carried for miles beyond the mountain's base.

After these first avalanches had come to rest, the canyons were almost choked, and at night the deposits they had left behind them glowed like embers. Had it been possible to look down upon the mountain from the air, every valley must have resembled a river of fire. On the plateau east of the mountain, more than a hundred square miles were blanketed with smoldering fragments.

Next day the volcano was again overwhelmed with avalanches, but its crown was hidden in folds of ash and the lower slopes were scarcely visible through the smoky haze. In the midst of this activity, noises of terrifying intensity came from the summit region. The mountain itself seemed to be breaking asunder, and the ground for miles around was violently shaken. The noises were quite different from the sudden, sharp blasts of explosions and from the peals of thunder continually rumbling. They sounded like the tumultuous roar that great rock slides make when they crash after a quarry blast, but magnified a thousandfold.

The activity died down as quickly as it had begun. Several days later, when the wind had cleared the air, the mountain was again revealed. The change in its form was one to stagger the imagination. The majestic ice-clad peak that had formerly dominated the landscape, rising in lofty

MOUNT MAZAMA JUST AFTER THE DESTRUCTION OF ITS SUMMIT

—From a painting by Paul Rockwood

grandeur above all the surrounding peaks, had disappeared. In its place was a stupendous caldron, between 5 and 6 miles wide and 4000 feet deep, enclosed by jagged cliffs. No words can convey the wild confusion of the scene. Jets of steam hissed and roared from countless fissures, their noise mingling with the din of rock slabs falling from the cliffs. Pungent smells of sulphur and smarting fumes of acid rose from the awful pit and clouds of dust-laden vapor tossed like curtains in the gusty wind. The floor of the colossal basin was a chaotic jumble of tremendous blocks, as if some Brobdingnagian hand had been at work shattering the mountain. Here and there were yawning gashes. Dozens of pools, some milky white, others dark green, and others of ochreous mud were boiling and spattering vigorously.

All that remained of the wide fields of ice that formerly crowned the peak were the small stumps, the beheaded remnants of three glaciers in Munson, Sun, and Kerr valleys. The remaining slopes of the mountain were dreary wastes of ashen gray. The deep glacial canyons were filled almost to the brim with pumice. Each one had become a "Valley of Ten Thousand Smokes," riddled with branching fissures from which acid fumes rose in seething clouds. Even decades later there were places where the pumice was still so hot that when rain fell upon it the surface was shrouded in steam. And for years the upper atmosphere was so charged with impalpable dust that all over the world the sky at sunrise and sunset was painted in brilliant colors. In distant lands men marveled at the lights.

The Growth of Wizard Island

THE VOLCANO had spent prodigious strength in the destruction of its summit and for a long time it lay exhausted. Gradually the pools on the floor of the caldron ceased to boil, and the discharge of steam died down. Trees began to return to the outer slopes of the mountain, spreading upward year by year. Though the volcano lay quiet it was not yet extinct, but only slumbering. Despite the vast amount of magma that had been blown from the underlying reservoir during the great eruptions, much still remained, and slowly it regathered energy. Finally, it developed enough pressure to force a passage through the shattered floor of the caldron. A cone of cinders, known as the Merriam Cone, 1300 feet high and a mile wide, arose near the north wall of the caldron. Fluid lava spread rapidly from its base to form an agitated "lake of fire." At night the lake disclosed a changing tracery of bright red bands. Where the gases escaped most readily, the lava was hotter and glowed a bright orange. Here and there blue flames of burning hydrogen danced across the surface. After several months the activity came to an end, and the "lake of fire" cooled to a black plain of solid lava. These events took place when Crater Lake was still very shallow.

When the next eruptions took place, the center of activity had moved toward the southwestern edge of the caldron. Lava piled on lava until a high and broad platform was built above the floor. When this had risen to the present level of the lake the quiet outpouring ceased for a time and gave place to more violent eruptions. Showers of red-hot ash and pasty lava clots were thrown into the air. Cooling in their flight, they fell to earth as cinder-like fragments, and, piling around the vent, they slowly built the cone of Wizard Island. The Indians living in the neighboring region were afraid to approach the mountain, for they could see the glowing projectiles rising high above the rim and could hear the roar of explosions from afar. They were alarmed by the ruddy canopy of clouds, afraid that it might prove only a prelude to eruptions as devastating as those recounted in their legends.

After the cone of "cinders" had been formed, the explosions ended and lava again poured from Wizard Island. Some of it oozed through the "cinders" near the top of the cone, and some rose to the floor of the small crater at the summit and congealed there as a plug to the feeding pipe, but most of the lava burst through cracks around the base of the cone and spread sluggishly toward the west until it almost reached the adjacent wall of the caldron. The crust of the lava was shattered into blocks and these were carried forward on the liquid material below. Before the first flows were completely solid, their blocky crusts were rucked into wavelike ridges by the onward pressure of those that followed. Today the curved ridges are emphasized by patches of snow and jade-green pools in the intervening hollows, and as we look down upon them from The Watchman we can picture the lavas still advancing and seem to hear the clatter of the jostling blocks. But this, the final act of Mount Mazama, happened almost a thousand years ago.

From the day when the caldron was first formed, pools of water had dotted the floor. And the pools deepened with every rain until they were all united into a single sheet of water. As the passing clouds unburdened themselves of their moisture, the level of the lake gradually rose. Four-fifths of the water fell directly into the lake as rain and snow; the remainder was supplied by small torrents cascading into the basin from the encircling cliffs. For a time the water level was higher than it is today, and the remains of diatoms, minute single-celled plants living in the lake, were deposited on the slopes of Wizard Island, 40 to 50 feet above the present surface. Even within the present century, the level has fallen approximately 13 feet.

Nowadays, the level is fairly constant, apart from seasonal fluctuations of a few feet. It is highest in the early summer when the snows are melting fast, and lowest at the end of the season. Otherwise, the amount of water added by rain, snow, and streams keeps pace with that lost by evaporation and by percolation through the walls.

PART TWO: THE EVIDENCE

The Setting of Crater Lake

WHEN WE arrived at the rim of the lake, we heard that one of the Ranger Naturalists of the Park Service staff was about to lead an auto-caravan trip to the summit of The Watchman, a high point on the western wall. When he told us that we should get a splendid view from there of how the lake is related to the neighboring volcanoes of the Cascade Range, we were delighted to join him.

Arrived at the lookout station, we could see how the slopes outside the rim slant away gently in all directions, and we were at once impressed by the fact that Crater Lake does indeed occupy the top of a decapitated mountain. Giving imagination play, we pictured the missing slopes continuing upward above the lake to an ice-clad peak.

"Except for the distant Klamath and Siskiyou mountains," the Naturalist said, "virtually all the wide panorama that we see from here is made up of volcanic rocks. We are in the heart of one of the most extensive volcanic provinces in the world. Intermittently, for the last 60 million years, volcanoes have been erupting in this region. The youngest volcanoes, those formed in the last 10 or 12 million years, are arranged in a long north–south belt that passes through Crater Lake. This belt, the 'High Cascades,' includes all the crowning peaks of the range. Far to the south, out of sight, rises Lassen Peak, which erupted in 1914–1917, and is the most recently active volcano in the United States. Closer to Crater Lake, we see the giant cones of Shasta, McLoughlin, and Union Peak, with many humbler volcanic peaks between. In the opposite direction stretches a magnificent series of huge, white-capped cones, continuing beyond the horizon to Adams, St. Helens, Rainier, and Baker. From one end in northern California to the other near Vancouver, in British Columbia, this chain of volcanoes has a length of about 500 miles. Yet, long as it is, it forms only a small fraction of the 'circle of fire' that surrounds the entire Pacific Ocean."

One member of the party, impressed by the thought that the ocean is encircled by volcanoes, asked for an explanation. It is easy to embarrass even a specialist by probing into fundamentals! The Naturalist, aware that the origins of volcanic action are still a matter for debate, answered with hesitation, "The rocks that make up the earth's crust around the Pacific have been disturbed for countless ages. The earthquakes which still affect this region are signs that the disturbances are not yet ended. Many new mountain ranges have been raised along the Pacific border within recent geologic times."

Before he could continue, someone interposed, "How do you know that the mountains have been raised? And what raises them?"

"Has everyone here heard of the shells of marine animals, of whale bones and the like, found embedded in rocks now far inland?" he asked. Most agreed that they had. "Then you will admit," he continued, "that those rocks must have been lifted from the sea. And, if you will accept my word for it, the geologist can tell approximately how many millions of years ago this took place by examining the fossil shells and bones and referring them to their proper place in the scale of evolution."

"But what has this to do with volcanoes?" the first speaker asked.

The Naturalist thought for a moment how best to reply to the difficult question. "You know," he said, "that in deep mines the temperature is far higher than at the surface. When oil wells are drilled, the drillers find that the temperature increases downward, on an average, 100° Fahrenheit per mile. If it were possible to bore a hole 40 miles deep, the rocks at the bottom would be found to have a temperature far above that at which they melt at the surface."

Again he was interrupted. "You mean," asked a timid old lady, "that at that depth all the rocks are molten?" The thought was rather alarming.

He assured her that this was not the case. "The vibrations caused by earthquakes show conclusively that for tens and even hundreds of miles below the surface the rocks are solid. The interior of the earth is as rigid as steel, because of the enormous weight of the overlying rocks. Forty miles down, the pressure on every square inch is not less than 100 tons. And the more a rock is subjected to pressure, the higher is the temperature necessary to melt it. Most geologists suppose that the earth's hot core is slowly cooling and shrinking. As it does so, the outer layers respond to fit it by bending and breaking. The rocky envelope crumples as the skin of a baked apple wrinkles when it cools."

Rather than confuse the issue, he added, "Whatever other causes are involved in the bending and breaking of the crust and the upheaval of mountains, the effect is to rearrange the load on the deep-seated material below. Where cracks are opened, the pressure may be so far reduced on parts of the hot core as to cause the rocks to melt. The rocks then change to red-hot, pasty 'magma,' and this stiff liquid finds its way upward along the cracks and escapes at the surface in the form of lava and ash. This is perhaps the chief way by which volcanoes are produced."

For a few moments nobody spoke, and it seemed to the Naturalist that his audience was either satisfied with the explanation or did not wish to continue the discussion further. But then a man in the rear questioned, "I come from Pennsylvania, in the heart of the Appalachian Mountains. You say that when mountains are upheaved, volcanoes are produced. How is it we have no volcanoes in Pennsylvania?"

This was not an audience to be trifled with. The Naturalist replied, "I'm sorry if I gave the impression that every mountain-building movement causes volcanic eruptions. It would be as false to say so as to say that all earthquakes are produced by volcanic action. Both are symptoms of an unstable crust. Often the crust is bent, broken, and raised without the removal of enough pressure on the hot core to result in melting. At other times, when part of the rocky core does melt, the liquid magma fails to reach the surface and solidifies far below. For instance, granites such as you have in the Appalachians, or those exposed in the wonderful valley of Yosemite, were formed by the cooling and solidification of magma at a depth of many miles. It is possible to see the granites today because, after millions of years, the combined attack of rain, rivers, ice, and snow has worn away the overlying materials."

Time was pressing and there was so much more to be seen that the Naturalist turned to point out other features of the landscape. He indicated that all the volcanoes of the High Cascades which are less than 10 or 12 million years old are still roughly conical in form, even though many have been greatly modified by erosion. And he told us that the rocks composing all of them are of exactly the same kinds as those in the walls of Crater Lake. He then pointed westward, to the country beyond the Rogue River.

"You will see," he said, "that the western part of the Cascade Range looks quite different from the High Cascades. Notice that the mountains to the west do not have simple conical shapes. They form an irregular 'sea of peaks and ridges,' separated by winding valleys. And yet the Western Cascades are also composed of volcanic rocks."

"Then why are there no volcanic cones?" someone asked.

"They were destroyed by erosion long ago," he answered. "The lavas and ashes were poured over that region millions of years before the High Cascade cones were formed. In fact, when the first of them was erupted, all this part of Oregon was a low, wooded, tropical plain.

Then, after these older volcanoes became extinct, the thick blanket of materials produced by their eruptions was raised by earth movements to form a mountain range. And throughout the long period when the High Cascade volcanoes were growing, this range was sculptured by rivers to give us the landscape we see today. In other words, the shapes of those distant mountains are not original volcanic forms, but are the product of erosion working among volcanic rocks."

Most of us had never thought of landscapes changing in this sense, nor were we accustomed to thinking in terms of millions of years. Yet if, as the Naturalist said, the rocks of the Western Cascades are volcanic, and if, as he assured us, the petrified remains of figs and palms have been found among them, it was clear that we had to abandon our ideas of permanence and accept the time scale of the geologist if we were to understand how the scenery was evolved.

We then turned to look in an easterly direction. What we saw there was a landscape utterly different from either the High or the Western Cascades. As far as the eye could see, there was an almost flat plateau above which rose steep-sided, mesalike mountains. Stimulated by what we had already learned, we asked our guide to explain the difference.

"You see to the east," he said, "part of what some people call the Great Interior Platform or the Columbia River Plateau. You are looking at a small part of an immense volcanic surface that spreads north into Washington, east into Idaho, and south into California, covering between 200,000 and 300,000 square miles."

Someone asked why no volcanic cones could be seen.

The Naturalist replied, "The lavas of this plateau country were erupted quite differently from those of the Cascade Range. Instead of flowing from more or less cylindrical pipes fed by chambers of molten rock a few miles below the surface, the plateau lavas rose from swarms of long cracks and were fed by supplies of molten rock from a vastly greater depth."

"Even so," the questioner interrupted, "I don't see why the lava didn't pile around the cracks and build a ridge over each. Why did it spread out so evenly?"

"Because it was far more fluid than the lavas erupted by the Cascade volcanoes. It spread rapidly from the cracks and flooded the country for miles around. The stiffer Cascade lavas, on the other hand, accumulated close to the feeding pipes and so built high cones."

"One last question," asked the inquiring one. "Can you tell us how old these plateau lavas are, compared with those of the Cascades?"

"Most of them were erupted approximately 15 to 20 million years ago, long after the volcanoes of the Western Cascades had started to form, but before any of the High Cascade volcanoes existed."

Our trip to the top of The Watchman had opened undreamt-of vistas. Now that we knew more about the relation of Crater Lake to the neighboring country, we were anxious for details about the growth of Mount Mazama itself.

Along the Rim Trail

As we descended the trail from The Watchman, the Naturalist, eager to hold our attention, turned the tables and asked, "Apart from the beauty of the coloring, what struck you most about the walls of Crater Lake?"

Several of us answered that their height and steepness were most impressive. But one in the party, perhaps guessing what was in the Naturalist's mind, said that what struck him particularly was the layered arrangement of the rocks. Pleased with the response, the Naturalist asked for an explanation; which was:

"You said yourself that the Cascade volcanoes were built by alternate eruptions of lava and volcanic fragments. I assume that the layers must have been laid down by successive eruptions."

"No doubt about it. Where do you think the source was?"

"It must have been high above the middle of the lake, because all the layers in the walls slope outward. The lava flows must have poured downhill from an opening or crater far above."

"Then you will agree that the gentle slopes around Crater Lake must originally have swept upward to a giant peak, just as the gentle slopes near the base of Shasta, Hood, and Rainier rise more and more steeply toward the summit?"

We all agreed. He then pointed toward the southeast wall of the lake. "You see those two deep notches on the far wall? One of them is Kerr Notch and the other, Sun Notch. The deep canyons which lead up to them cannot always have ended so abruptly, but must once have extended much higher. By the way, is there anything peculiar about the shapes of the notches?"

It was not long before someone answered, "Yes, they seem to be remarkably symmetrical, like a letter U."

"Exactly," said the Naturalist, "and that shape is typical of valleys gouged by moving glaciers. On the other hand, when you look up or down a river valley, don't you see the sides descending to the floor like the sides of a letter V?"

He did not wait for a reply, but continued, "At one time Sun and Kerr notches were filled to the brim with thick glaciers, and in order to supply such a vast amount of ice there must have been a great snow field at a much higher elevation."

Having made his point, he led us to the brink of the cliffs. "We speak of this as Crater Lake," he said, "but actually this is not a crater at all in the strict sense." He half apologized for the technicality. "Properly speaking, this should be called a 'caldera,' a name adopted by geologists from the Portuguese name for a caldron."

"But why?" came the question.

"To be exact," the Naturalist answered, "a crater is an opening at the top of a volcanic pipe, and it is rarely more than a mile wide—usually less than half a mile. It is the funnel-shaped or cylindrical vent through which a volcano erupts its products. A caldera is a vastly bigger depression, generally several miles across."

Following the rim of the caldera, we arrived shortly at Discovery Point, whence Hillman first saw the lake in 1853. After a brief search, we found, on the very brink of the cliffs, the polished and scratched surface of lava here depicted (in the plate facing page 18, lower picture).

"This," said our guide, "is a kind of calling card bearing the signature of a glacier that once passed this way. Not only that, but the scratches tell us in what direction the ice was moving. They were made by fragments of rock frozen into the bottom of the ice as it crept down the mountainside."

As he was explaining how the fine rock dust embedded in the ice polished even the most resistant surface, and how, when the ice melted, this rock waste was left behind as a moraine, a man who had been peering over the edge of the cliff called excitedly, "Here's another polished slab of lava about 40 feet down."

Though the polish was not so well preserved as that on the slab at our feet, there was no doubt that it must have been produced in the same way. The glacier that polished the lower lava must therefore have melted and disappeared before the upper lava was erupted. Then, when the surface of this upper lava had solidified, it was polished by a second glacier creeping down the sides of the volcano.

He then showed us a map (here reproduced on p. 51) on which he had plotted the position and direction of all

SOUTHEAST WALL OF CRATER LAKE, AND PART OF WIZARD ISLAND. FROM LEFT TO RIGHT: KERR NOTCH, DUTTON CLIFF, SUN NOTCH, APPLEGATE AND GARFIELD PEAKS, AND MUNSON VALLEY

WIZARD ISLAND

CRATER LAKE FROM THE WEST

—*Photo Washington National Guard*

the glacial scratches on the caldera rim and walls. "You will see," he said, "that scratched rocks can be found almost everywhere along the rim, even on many of the highest points. You can find them, for example, on the

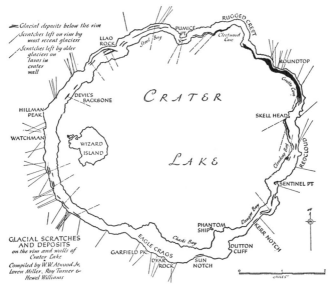

Glacial scratches and deposits on the rim and walls of Crater Lake.

high part of the rim between Garfield and Applegate peaks. Hence, the last glaciers must have covered virtually the entire volcano, filling the valleys and spreading across the intervening spurs."

When he asked if there was anything distinctive about the directions of the scratches on the rim, one member of the party replied that while most of them were arranged like the spokes of a wheel, many did not point toward the center of the lake. We could see no special significance in the remark, but after a few moments the Naturalist explained: "If the old peak of Mount Mazama had been a perfect cone, the glaciers would have spread uniformly from the summit in all directions and the scratches would point to a single source. Since many of the scratches, especially near Hillman Peak and Roundtop, do not point to a common center, we can only suppose that instead of being a simple cone the vanished part of Mount Mazama must have been complex in outline. There must have been smaller cones on the sides of the main cone [see frontispiece, picturing the mountain before its destruction], just as Shastina rises from the side of Shasta. These minor cones deflected some of the glaciers sweeping down from the central peak. That is why the directions of many ice scratches are so irregular."

The apparently futile task of plotting ice scratches had, surprisingly, thrown light on the shape of a vanished mountain.

For some time the talk turned from geology to a discussion of the trees and flowers along the rim and it was only after we had returned to the parapet of the Sinnott Memorial, not far from the Lodge, that our attention was again directed to the rocks. Field glasses were already arranged for our convenience and focused on points of special interest. We looked first at the massive face of Dutton Cliff, where the caldera wall reaches a height of almost

2000 feet. The whole precipice was striped with irregular reddish bands.

"The dark layers you see between the red," said the Naturalist, "are lava flows. Some of the red bands are composed of volcanic ash, but most of them are the slaggy, clinkery crusts of the lavas themselves. While the flows

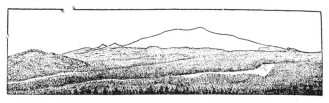

Mount Mazama from the southwest. The two peaks on the west (left) slope are the parasitic cones of The Watchman and Hillman Peak. The peak on the right is Garfield. In the foreground, Castle Creek Canyon.

were still moving, hot gases escaped through the crusts, causing them to be oxidized and become rusty."

He pointed to the deep gully beyond the eastern end of the parapet. "For about 80 feet downward from the rim," he said, "you see a mass of boulders embedded in sand. Exactly the same type of deposit occurs in the Camp Grounds and around the Lodge. It was left there by a powerful glacier that once continued down Munson Valley, past the Government Headquarters, into the canyon of Annie Creek."

Someone asked if the brighter brown, yellow, and pale gray bouldery layers farther down the gully were also left by glaciers.

"No," he replied, "those are the products of violent explosions. The fine material between the blocks is not sand, but volcanic ash. During periods when the volcano was quiet, the lava in the feeding pipes solidified to a great depth. When the pressure of the gases imprisoned below increased sufficiently, they blasted a way to the surface, shattered the plugs, and hurled blocks and fine ash for miles around. Most of the materials were already solid before they were erupted. If you care to examine this particular type of material at close quarters, take the trail up Garfield Peak, where you can see several layers interbedded among the lavas."

"You imply," said one of the party, "that there were times when explosions produced other types of material."

"Yes," he answered, directing us to look at the white banks of material above and below Llao Rock and on Redcloud Cliff. "Especially during the last stages of the volcano's history, the material blown out was chiefly in the form of gas-rich magma, and it was hurled high above the mountain in red-hot, pasty fragments. Distended by the escaping gases, each fragment fell to earth as a piece of white, frothy glass. This light, foamy material or pumice was blown out in prodigious quantities in the final eruptions that led to the destruction of Mount Mazama, and covers thousands of square miles to the north and east of here."

Just before the Naturalist left, we asked him about the Devil's Backbone, a conspicuous wall-like mass of rock that extends from the water's edge to the rim of the caldera, cutting clean across the layers of lava and ash. (See upper picture in plate facing p. 66.)

"It is the largest of the 'dikes'—as geologists call them— around Crater Lake," he replied. "All told, there are fifteen or sixteen of them, and most of them point approximately toward the middle of the lake. They were formed when the pressure of the molten rock, pushing upward from the feeding chamber, was strong enough to crack the entire volcano. The molten material forced into the cracks cooled to produce unusually hard, dense rocks. Long afterward, when the top of Mount Mazama disappeared, the dense fillings of the cracks, being more resistant than the bordering materials, were sculptured into relief and so stand out like buttresses."

By Boat Round the Lake

PERHAPS no single trip in any of our National Parks can give greater pleasure or rouse a livelier interest in the interpretation of landscape than the trip by launch around the edge of Crater Lake. Under ideal conditions, it affords the visitor an opportunity of seeing the inner framework of a huge volcano and of learning how it was formed.

Shortly after descending the zigzag trail from the rim to the Boat Landing, our journey began. The water was smooth and mirrored the walls like glass. In a few minutes, we were close to the shores of Wizard Island. Here, the Naturalist told us, is where the last fires of Mount Mazama burned. The black wilderness of rugged lavas, topped by the somber cone of cinders, left a deep impression on our minds. We pictured the cone blowing out red-hot fragments and the lava oozing from its sides. Someone asked the Naturalist if the island would ever erupt again.

"Nobody can say," he replied. "Volcanoes may sleep for hundreds or even thousands of years, and then suddenly awaken. But there are no hot springs or hot gas vents in the Park, and there are no records of volcanic earthquakes to suggest the stirring of molten rock underground. Still, it would be rash to say that the volcano is dead and not just slumbering." Then, as if to calm our fears, he added, "Studies of other volcanoes in the Cascade Range lead us to think that those which are not yet dead are fast approaching extinction."

As we rounded the island and passed through Skell Channel, the Naturalist pointed to the lookout tower on The Watchman. "The thick lava flow which forms The Watchman did not pour from the summit of Mount Mazama," he said, "but from the sides of the volcano through an opening which once existed under the lookout tower itself."

Soon we were skirting the beautifully colored cliffs under Hillman Peak, where the drab tints of the lava flows change to more pleasing shades of red, orange, brown, and yellow. We asked why the walls are so much brighter here than elsewhere.

"If you will look at Hillman Peak," the Naturalist said, "you will see that the layers of lava and ash slope more steeply there than elsewhere. A steep-sided cone must once have risen from the gentler slopes of Mount Mazama at this point. When the top of the mountain was destroyed, half the Hillman cone vanished with it, and what you see now is the remaining half in section. If you care to scramble among those brightly colored crags just below the rim, you can see the lava filling of the pipe through which the Hillman cone was fed. While the cone was still erupting, hot gases and liquids rose through the feeding pipe. There may well have been boiling pools at the surface. In any event, the rising liquids and gases decomposed the rocks and left a coating of iron oxides on them."

"I noticed yellow and brown tints among the rocks on Garfield Peak. Were they formed in the same way?" someone asked.

"Yes," he answered, "Most of the brighter coloring on the walls of Crater Lake was produced by hot springs and hot gases acting on the lavas, and the main pigment everywhere is iron oxide. The delicate coloring of the lavas in the Grand Canyon of the Yellowstone and round the boiling pools near Lassen Peak was formed in the same manner."

Passing close to the Devil's Backbone, we soon arrived in front of Llao Rock. To appreciate the magnitude and form of the enormous flow, we stood well out from shore. From out on the lake, it seemed to have the shape of a giant bird with wings outspread. On either side of the thick central body the lava rapidly tapered to the edges. (See plate facing p. 67.)

> Great bird of fire, cold now, and gray, and lone,
> Ten thousand years have seen you never wake,
> Ten thousand more shall know your breast of stone,
> Brooding far up above the silent lake.
>
> MOLL, *Blue Interval*

"You will see," said our guide, "that the central part of the lava occupies what was once a roughly U-shaped valley. From what you have seen elsewhere, I think you will agree that the valley looks like one sculptured by ice. As a matter of fact, we know quite definitely that the lava does fill a glacial valley, because ice-scratched boulders are embedded in the bottom of the flow. We also know that the lava did not pour from the summit of Mount Mazama, but was erupted from a crater on the valley floor, for the feeding pipe is exposed beneath the base of the flow. This is what must have happened: first, glaciers carved a broad valley, and then, after the ice disappeared, explosions blasted a crater through the valley floor. Lava welled upward, piled higher and higher, and finally spilled across the rims of the valley onto the surrounding flats."

"Why is it that this lava is so much thicker than all the others?" asked a man in the stern of the boat.

"Probably for two reasons," the Naturalist answered. "The flows which poured from the summit of the volcano were generally less bulky, and, being more fluid, they spread in thinner sheets. Except for this Llao flow and three others which we shall see later, one in Cleetwood Cove and two on Redcloud Cliff, all the lavas on the walls of Crater Lake are of andesite—so called from their resemblance to the principal type of lava erupted by the volcanoes of the Andes in South America. In fact, Mount Mazama had grown almost to its full height before erupting any other kind of material. The Llao, Cleetwood, and Redcloud lavas are composed of dacite. They contain more silica and alkalis, and less lime, iron, and magnesia than the andesites. Because of these differences, the dacite lavas were more pasty. They moved sluggishly and solidified before they had traveled far. For instance, this Llao dacite, though it is more than a thousand feet thick, was so pasty that it only flowed about a mile downhill before it was chilled to volcanic glass or obsidian."

As we continued northward across Steel Bay, we saw two conspicuous dikes. The one nearer Llao Rock can be traced up the wall for about 300 feet, maintaining a width of about 12 feet, until it suddenly flares at the top into a large, bulbous flow of lava. The other dike expands upward gradually from the water's edge until it merges into a horizontal sheet of lava.

"The manner in which these vertical dikes pass upward into horizontal flows," the Naturalist explained, "shows that from time to time lava burst to the surface through cracks in the side of the volcano instead of spilling from the crater at the summit. Probably many lavas on the lower slopes of the volcano were fed through similar cracks which are still concealed."

Soon we were rounding Pumice Point, so called on account of the long white bank of pumice which forms its upper half.

"At the bottom of the pumice," said the Naturalist, "there is a layer of glacial boulders and sand resting on ice-scratched lava. Fifty to 70 feet higher, within the pumice, there is a second layer of glacial material covered by a thin sheet of old soil. And just below the rim, but still within the pumice, there is a third layer of glacial boulders. Looking from here, you would never suspect any of this variation. Yet few parts of the caldera wall give us more vivid evidence of the alternation of glacial and volcanic action. Three times the glaciers advanced down this side of the volcano; three times they retreated, and at the time of one retreat they left the slopes bare long enough for plants to gain a foothold. Each retreat was followed by colossal eruptions of pumice."

As we continued eastward he told us that on one of the

small, rocky points jutting into the lake, no more than 20 feet above the water, the crust of the lowest lava flow is marked by well-preserved ice scratches. A few moments later the boatman turned off the motor and we glided into Cleetwood Cove, one of the most beautiful and most intensely blue of all the bays that indent the shore.

Pointing to the north wall of the cove, the Naturalist said, "This is the only place on the walls of Crater Lake where the rocks are not arranged in layers. Instead, you see a dark, rough tongue of lava extending from the rim to the water's edge. I'd be interested to know what you think of it."

A young man who had evidently had some training in geology remarked, "The lava must have poured down the wall from somewhere along the rim, and in order for it to do so the top of the mountain must already have disappeared. In other words, Crater Lake was here when the lava was erupted."

"That is exactly what I thought when I first saw it," answered the Naturalist. "For a long time this was known as the Cleetwood 'backflow,' because it gives the impression of having poured back into the caldera. But now we know that it is really an 'upflow.'"

"I confess that I don't follow you," said the young man.

"What we see here," the Naturalist continued, "is the filling of an inclined pipe up which lava rose and broke through the sides of Mount Mazama. It was not until long afterward, when the top of the mountain disappeared, that the pipe was revealed. The lava which escaped from the pipe to the slopes of the volcano was extremely pasty and its crust cooled to glistening black glass. Borne along by the sluggish creep of the molten material underneath, the glassy crust was shattered into jagged pinnacles. Even from here you can see the sunlight glancing on the bristling spires along the rim. Little wonder we call this part of the rim the Rugged Crest."

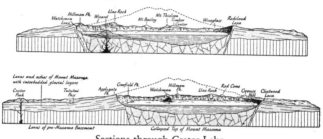

Sections through Crater Lake.

Rounding Palisade Point, we approached the imposing cliffs under Roundtop. Just before we reached them, the Naturalist drew our attention to a place a short distance up the wall, from which water was seeping.

"Wherever you see water seeping from the walls round Crater Lake," he said, "it is a pretty good indication of the presence of glacial materials. Rain water and melting snow percolate through cracks in the lavas until they come to a glacial layer rich in clay. This checks the downward flow and forces the water to the surface in the form of springs. If you were to examine this particular seepage you would find the water oozing from layers of sand and gravel containing glacial boulders."

"You mean that this is an old glacial moraine," some-one remarked.

"No, I don't," he said. "If this were a moraine, the deposits would not be so well layered. In fact, they would be a chaotic mixture of fragments of all sizes. The layering and the presence of glacial boulders show that the sands and gravels were laid down by rivers pouring from the ends of glaciers that once existed higher up the mountain."

As we passed under the cliffs of Roundtop, he asked the boatman to slow down a little. "I wish we had time to land here," he said, "and climb to the bottom of this flow. I could show you where the lava, while it was still molten, picked up ice-scratched boulders from the underlying moraine. And then I could take you to the top of the cliffs and show you that after the lava solidified, the ice readvanced and polished the crust."

A few moments later we passed by the pumice slide called the Wineglass and were skirting the shores of Grotto Cove. Just before we reached Skell Head, the Naturalist pointed to a smaller promontory and said that ice scratches are preserved on the top of the lowest lava flow, only 30 feet above the lake.

Our next stop was in Cloudcap Bay, under the very high triangular lava cliff, Redcloud.

"I hope you don't object to my asking questions," he said, "but what do you make of this great lava flow? How do you explain the fact that the sides slope together like the sides of a letter V and cut across all the other layered lavas?"

"You were telling us yesterday," replied the young geologist, "that glacial valleys are U-shaped whereas river valleys are V-shaped. My guess is that this thick flow poured down an old river valley on the side of the volcano."

"Things are not always what they seem," said the Naturalist, apologizing for the triteness. "What you see here is a slice through a funnel-shaped crater that was blasted through the side of Mount Mazama and later filled with a high mound of pasty dacite. The bottom of the V marks the actual outlet through which the lava rose."

A little beyond the center of Cloudcap Bay we paused again, so that our guide might explain what was to be seen in the cliffs.

"This is perhaps the most interesting part of the entire caldera wall," the Naturalist said. "Between the edge of the lake and the caldera rim there are no fewer than seven distinct layers of glacial material. Let me indicate them. Under each of the three lowest lava flows you see a bench covered with loose material and dotted with bushes. The presence of the vegetation is caused by water seeping from glacial material under each flow. Probably these are the oldest glacial deposits to be seen anywhere inside the park. When they were left here by melting ice, Mount Mazama was still in its infancy and only a few thousand feet high."

He pointed to two other glacial layers higher up the wall, but they were impossible to distinguish properly from the boat. "The two highest layers," he continued, "lie on top of the topmost lava. One of them is invisible from here, but the other forms the pale gray band between the white layers just inside the rim."

After he had pointed out this eloquent evidence of the repeated advance and retreat of the glaciers on the sides of the growing volcano, someone asked, "What is that curiously carved, delicately tinted crag about two-thirds the distance up the wall?"

"We call that the Cottage Rock or sometimes the Crater Castle," he replied. "It has been sculptured by rain wash and frost from a thick mass of pumice. The delicate pink, orange, and cream colors were caused by hot gases escaping from the pumice while it was still hot."

Rounding Sentinel Point, we passed close to a vertical dike and entered Danger Bay. When the south face of the point came into full view, we looked back and saw the lava-filled funnel through which the topmost flow was erupted. Then, as we approached Kerr Notch, we heard the sound of cataracts and saw from the lush vegetation that the streams were fed by a curved line of springs a short distance up the wall. A few moments later we were at the foot of Dutton Cliff, and we could see another line of springs discharging water into the lake from halfway up the wall. We felt sure that each of these lines marked the presence of a glacial layer among the volcanic rocks.

A cormorant flew overhead from the direction of the Phantom Ship, and soon we were circling the rocky island itself, admiring its strange sculpture.

"How do you account for this peculiar formation?" someone asked.

"Notice that the Ship consists of two kinds of rock," the Naturalist responded. "The sides are chiefly composed of pale green volcanic ash, whereas the mimic sails consist mostly of a dark brown to black rock. The darker rock was produced by solidification of molten material forced into a vertical crack cutting the paler ash."

"Do you mean that the sails of the ship are part of a dike?"

"Exactly. And it is because the dike is composed of resistant, fine-grained rock that the Ship has been able to survive. Notice also which way the dike points. If you look about a third of the way up the adjacent wall of the caldera, you will see a bold, triangular cliff. That represents the filling of still another volcanic pipe. And this dike on the Phantom Ship is an offshoot from that."

The breeze seldom ruffles the water before noon, but this morning it was beginning early. The reflections were becoming blurred. Crossing Chaski Bay, we saw where an enormous mass of lava had slid down to the water from the cliffs above. We skirted by the Eagle Crags, where bald and golden eagles sometimes make their nests. A few minutes later our journey was ended. As we climbed back along the zigzag trail to the rim, we stopped time and again to look back at the caldera walls to remind ourselves of the long story they had told, and as we watched the play of lights on the lake we were filled with a new and deeper feeling for its beauty.

—*Photo Washington National Guard*

SOUTHWEST WALL OF CRATER LAKE, AND WIZARD ISLAND. IN THE MIDDLE DISTANCE (*left*), DEVIL'S BACKBONE AND LLAO ROCK. IN THE FARTHER DISTANCE (*center*), TIMBER CRATER AND (*left*) PINNACLE OF MOUNT THIELSEN

—*Photo Washington National Guard*

EAST WALL OF CRATER LAKE, WITH MOUNT SCOTT BEYOND

West Wall of Crater Lake; Llao Rock in Center

Valleys of 10,000 Smokes

WE HAD climbed The Watchman, driven along the Rim Road, and made the launch trip round the lake, and were anxious to see as much more as possible during our brief stay. We turned to the Naturalist for suggestions.

"If you care for an even better view of the lake and the surrounding country than you had yesterday from The Watchman," he said, "you should climb the trail to the top of Mount Scott. From there you will see as fine a panorama as from any peak in Oregon. Or you might climb to the top of Union Peak."

"What would we see on the way to Union Peak?" we asked.

"The first part of the trip," he answered, "is across the ice-sculptured lava slopes of the volcano, which, by the way, is older than Mount Mazama. Beyond the end of the Fire Road you take a trail across the ashes which originally formed a cone inside the crater. And finally you come to the summit pinnacle, a miniature Matterhorn. This is the lava filling of the central pipe of the volcano, which still stands because of its superior resistance to erosion. Incidentally, at the top some of the lava has been fused to bubbly green glass by strokes of lightning."

"Have you any other suggestions?"

"Yes. If you care to see one of the many so-called 'cinder cones,' you cannot do better than climb Red Cone. There you can see splendid examples of volcanic bombs, a few of them as much as 6 feet long. Some are spindle-shaped, others almond- and pear-shaped, and some are twisted like rope. They were blown out as red-hot clots of lava and shaped by spinning through the air. You can also see flows of lava that oozed through the 'cinders' near the top of the cone."

We were anxious to see more of the pumice blown out by the great eruptions which led to the destruction of the top of Mount Mazama.

"In that case," he continued, "you should certainly see Godfrey Glen; or, better still, the Pinnacles on Sand Creek. I'm sorry that I can't join you this afternoon, but let me introduce you to my friend here. He has been studying the geology of the park lately and happens to be going to the Pinnacles this afternoon to do some work."

The geologist kindly offered to act as our guide, and after lunch we started. As we drove from the rim to Government Headquarters, he pointed to the roadcuts and the hummocky ground on either side. "We are now crossing the bouldery moraines left by the Munson Valley glacier, one of the last to survive on the mountain," he said. "At one time this glacier continued for miles down Annie Creek Canyon and may almost have reached Fort Klamath."

"How can you tell?" we asked.

"Because moraines like these lie under the pumice in the bed of Annie Creek at least as far downstream as the south boundary of the park."

At the Government Headquarters we turned left along the Rim Road, and after traveling about three miles came to Tututni Pass. We parked our cars by the roadside and

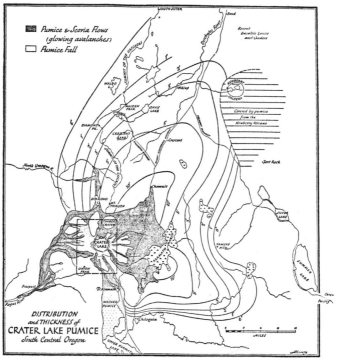

Map of pumice deposits around Crater Lake.

the geologist took from his pocket the map which is reproduced on this page.

"The Naturalist tells me that you are interested in the materials blown out by the last great eruptions of Mount

Mazama," he said. "I'm glad you are, because they hold the key to the origin of Crater Lake itself. Let me remind you briefly of what happened. Like most great eruptions, they began mildly and gradually increased in intensity to the climax. During the opening activity, the liquid magma frothed up the volcanic pipe and was blown high into the air in the form of light pumice. First, the wind blew the pumice to the east, and then, as the eruptions grew more violent, the pumice was blown more and more toward the northeast. It fell from the air in showers, falling on hill and valley alike. For that reason, we speak of the products of these early eruptions as those of the 'pumice fall.' Later, the activity became still more violent. Frothy magma rose from the depths with ever greater speed and volume. Finally, most of it was no longer blown high above the mountain and carried away by the wind, but boiled over the rim of the crater as boiling milk will froth from a pan, and swept down the mountainsides with amazing speed. We speak of the deposits left by these later eruptions as those of the glowing avalanches. This afternoon, I'd like to show you how we know what happened and how we can distinguish the two kinds of pumice."

He unfolded the map and we could see at once why he said that during the early eruptions the pumice was blown to the east and northeast by the winds.

"You will see from the map," he went on, "that very little pumice fell to the south and west of the volcano. In fact, it would have been perfectly safe to watch the eruptions from the sides of Union Peak. An area of more than 5000 square miles was buried under the pumice to a depth of more than 6 inches. An even greater area was covered by fine dust. Mazama ash has been traced at least 600 miles to the north of Crater Lake and more than 500 miles to the east. If any of you drive north when you leave, you'll notice the pumice in the roadcuts becomes steadily thinner and the fragments themselves become steadily smaller the farther you go."

"I understand why you say that the winds were blowing to the east and northeast," someone remarked, "but what I fail to see is how you know that the wind was blowing east at first and then switched to the northeast. And how can you tell that the eruptions grew more and more violent?"

"From studying roadcuts and digging pits," the geologist answered, "we know that in general the fragments of pumice become larger from the bottom of the deposit upward to the surface. This implies that the strength of the eruptions increased more or less steadily." We agreed; and he went on, "Besides, we find that to the east of Crater Lake the fragments of pumice are on the whole much smaller than they are at the same distance to the northeast. This suggests that by the time large lumps were being blown out the winds had already veered to the northeast."

"What is the size of the largest lump you've found?" we asked.

"On the side of Timber Crater, about 5 miles northeast of the rim of the lake, I found one piece 8 inches across," he replied. "Forty miles away in the same direction, there are few pieces more than 3 inches across. Seventy or 80 miles away, pieces more than an inch across are rare. And so it goes."

He led us to a deep cut at a bend of the road.

"This is as good a place as any," he said, "to see what the material of the pumice fall looks like." Each of us seized a handful. "Notice how light it is," he continued. "The pumice is so full of bubbles that it will float on water. It consists chiefly of finely spun, frothy volcanic glass produced from effervescing droplets of magma."

He passed around a magnifying glass. "Embedded in the glass you will see many small crystals. Some are clear and colorless, and others resemble shiny black needles. The clear ones are feldspar; the darker ones are hornblende, augite, and hypersthene. Few of the crystals are more than a tenth of an inch long, but all told they make up between 10 and 15 per cent of the total volume. I tell you this because, strangely enough, it has a distinct bearing on the origin of Crater Lake. These crystals were floating in the liquid magma before the eruptions began and while it was still inside the reservoir beneath Mount Mazama."

Someone remarked that he could see other fragments mingled with the light pumice which did not seem to be crystals, but small chips of lava.

"I'm glad you mentioned that," the geologist said. "Those dark chips are actually bits of old lava blown from the top of Mount Mazama together with the pumice.

Being much heavier, they tended to fall from the air closer to the source.

"How large are they close to the lake?" we asked.

"On Timber Crater, where I found the largest pieces of pumice, a few old rock fragments measure as much as 2 inches across," he answered. "But the size and proportion of the lava chips mingled with the pumice diminish rapidly as you go farther away. All told, they make up only about 4 per cent of the entire pumice fall."

"And how much pumice fell from the air?" we asked.

"Between 7 and 9 cubic miles," he answered.

We got back into the cars and did not stop again until we reached the Pinnacles on Sand Creek. (See plate facing p. 87.) Here the walls of the canyon bristle with slender pillars. As we stood wondering how the pillars were formed, the geologist approached, map in hand.

"If you entered the Park along the rim of Annie Creek Canyon, or from Medford along the rim of Castle Creek Canyon, you must already have seen deposits like these," he began. "Every canyon round Crater Lake is full of them. These are the deposits left by glowing avalanches."

He spread out the map so that we could see their distribution.

"You can see from this," he went on, "that the avalanches of pumice which rushed down from the top of Mount Mazama were confined to the valleys. Pouring from the mouths of the valleys, they spread in wide sheets over the plateau east of here. We never find their deposits on the ridges. On the other hand, the pumice blown out by the earlier eruptions, because it fell like rain from the air, covers hill and valley alike. That is one simple way of distinguishing between the two kinds of pumice."

"It seems to me," said a member of the party, "that the pumice here is much coarser than the materials we just saw, which, you say, fell from the air."

"To be sure," he replied. "These avalanches had such tremendous power that they were able to carry large lumps for amazing distances. I once talked to a man who was excavating pumice at Beaver Marsh, on the Dalles-California highway, 20 miles in an air line from the top of Mount Mazama. He told me that a few days before he had actually removed a lump of pumice 14 feet long. And I myself have seen several lumps in the same place which measured more than 6 feet across."

"It occurs to me," said another, "that when I came from Medford I saw thousands of big pumice lumps in the roadcuts. I remember because my wife picked up a lump about a yard across and we were surprised to find how light it was."

"You are perfectly right," said the geologist. "The glowing avalanches that raced down the west side of Mount Mazama poured into the valley of the Rogue and traveled a distance of about 35 miles. Even at the end, near the village of McLeod, there are pumice lumps more than a foot in diameter."

What he said next seemed at first like a contradiction, but he added an explanation of it. "Though the avalanche deposits contain a far greater number of lumps, and much larger ones, than those in the pumice fall, they are also much richer in fine, flourlike dust. The reason is this: The winds sifted out the fine dust from the pumice blown into the air and carried it for hundreds of miles. On the other hand, when the glowing avalanches rushed down the mountain, hugging the ground, the lumps were continually bombarding each other and being smashed. The lumps themselves were white-hot and many were shattered from within by the violent expansion of gases. It was because of internal explosions and the rapid expansion of hot gases that the avalanches were able to move so swiftly and so far. The wind had no chance to carry off the fine dust."

He asked if anyone expected to return to Medford after leaving the Park. Most of us planned to return to Klamath Falls, but one man said that he was almost certainly going back to Medford.

"If you do," said the geologist, "don't fail to drive a mile or two along the Diamond Lake highway above its junction with the Medford road. You'll see charcoal logs embedded in the avalanche deposits. As the glowing pumice swept into the forests, the trees were set on fire and slowly carbonized. So far, we have only found one charred tree standing upright in the position of growth. Most of the trees, in spite of their large size, were felled by the onrush of the avalanches."

"What kind of trees were they?" we asked.

"Exactly like those now living there," he answered; "pines, cedars, and an occasional Douglas fir."

"I don't see any in the pumice here," someone remarked.

"No," he said, "there are none. In fact, we seldom find any charred wood in the pumice within the park. Practically all of it lies at lower elevations."

"Then the trees on the higher slopes of the volcano must have been quite scattered," a woman in the party suggested.

We could control our interest in the slender pinnacles no longer, and asked for an explanation.

"Remember," he said, "that before the great eruptions began, the canyons around Crater Lake were not the narrow gorges we see today, but deep, rock-walled troughs, many of them a mile or more in width. When the avalanches came to rest, these wide valleys were choked with pumice. For several nights afterward the pumice must have glowed like the embers of a fire. Deep down, the pumice was so hot that tens of years passed before it was cool. Meanwhile, acid fumes and jets of steam rose up through cracks to the surface. Each canyon was a "Valley of Ten Thousand Smokes," like the famous valley near Katmai in Alaska which was deluged by hot pumice in 1912. It must have been a strange and moving sight. Wherever hot gases rose, they altered the pumice, staining it with red and brown oxides of iron. At the same time, streams were beginning to carve the present gorges."

He pointed to several of the slender columns, asking us to notice the cracks running up their sides.

"Many of these pillars are hollow inside," he said. "On the walls of Castle Creek there are some which have a central tube several feet across. The cracks and tubes mark the passageways up which the hot gases escaped to the surface. In a way the pillars are 'fossil gas vents.' And they stand out because the pumice bordering the cracks was hardened by the gases. As rain, wind, and frost sculptured the canyon walls, the more resistant parts were etched into relief. In time all the pillars you see now will disappear and new ones will be carved."

A member of our party who was taking colored pictures remarked that just inside the canyon rim there was a distinct brick-red layer.

"That layer," the geologist explained, "was also reddened by escaping gases. In fact, thousands of years ago the surface of the pumice must have been streaked with brilliant incrustations."

"How do you account for the fact that the lower half of the canyon walls is white and the upper half smoke-gray?" the photographer asked.

"To understand that," said our guide, "you must try to picture the conditions in the chamber under the volcano before the eruptions began. During the preceding period of rest the liquid magma in the chamber was undergoing slow changes. Light, frothy liquid was accumulating near the top while most of the crystals in the liquid settled toward the bottom. When, finally, the pressure of the gases became too great for the roof of the chamber to withstand, the light, frothy liquid near the top was blown out as pumice. Not until this was exhausted did the heavier and darker liquid, with its more numerous crystals, escape.

That, briefly, is why we see the dark material overlying the light in the canyons. You will notice the same arrangement on the walls of Godfrey Glen and Castle Creek."

"How much material was laid down by these glowing avalanches?" someone asked.

"At most, about 8 cubic miles," he answered. "Not all of that is pumice, however. Mingled with the pumice are fragments of old rock torn from the former top of the volcano. In fact, there is far more old rock among the glowing avalanches than in the pumice that fell in showers from the air. However, the strange thing is that the fragments are small. Considering the tremendous scale of the eruptions, you would think that gigantic blocks would have been torn from the top of the mountain. But, actually, almost all the old rock chips measure less than half an inch across, and there are few that are more than 3 inches long. Even on the rim of Crater Lake it is hard to find pieces more than a yard across. You'll see that this has an important bearing on the question of how the top of the mountain disappeared. But I'll leave that for the Naturalist to explain when you get back."

We thanked him for his kindness. It was obvious that he was anxious to be at work. The last we saw of him, he was in a cloud of dust as he scrambled down the pumice bank, brandishing his hammer. We looked into the peaceful canyon and at the graceful pillars, and thought how different the landscape must have been when it was still one of the "Valleys of Ten Thousand Smokes."

How the Mountaintop Fell

From the moment when we first saw Crater Lake, the question of how the caldera was formed had risen repeatedly in our minds. Obviously, forces of stupendous strength were involved. A mighty mountain had been wrecked, but the manner in which it was destroyed still baffled us. When we met the Naturalist again, we turned to him for an explanation.

"Just before the top of the volcano disappeared," he said, "it was close to 12,000 feet high. Altogether, 15 cubic miles of the volcano have vanished. There are only three ways in which this could possibly have happened: the mountain may have been destroyed by explosion, by collapse, or by a combination of the two." He paused for a moment, and then asked, "Does anyone care to express an opinion on the question?"

After some hesitation, one man replied, "I don't feel qualified to judge, but offhand it seems to me that explosion is the most likely explanation. After all, we've seen tremendous quantities of pumice around the lake. The idea of collapse is hard for me to grasp. How could a mountain collapse? Where would it go to?"

The Naturalist did not answer the questions immediately, but said, "At first sight, explosion does seem the most reasonable explanation. But pause for a moment and try to visualize how enormous a volume is represented by

1 5 cubic miles. Suppose, for example, that when the explosions took place the fragments fell evenly on the slopes around Crater Lake for a distance of 5 miles from the rim. They would form a sheet of blocks more than 500 feet thick. Actually, the fragments would not fall uniformly over the mountain, but most of them would accumulate near the source. The largest blocks would pile up close to the caldera, while the fine dust would be carried for scores of miles by the wind. Probably a layer of blocks 1000 or more feet thick would be formed along the rim itself. You know as well as I do that no such layer exists."

The man who favored the idea of explosion interrupted. "Certainly," he said, "there is no thick layer of blocks along the rim; but I did see several cuts on the Rim Road that were chiefly made up of blocks."

"To be sure," agreed the Naturalist, "there are many patches of blocks, but most of them are the remains of bouldery glacial moraines and not products of explosion. Instead of a vast sheet of blocks blown from the top of the volcano, what you see for miles beyond the rim is an almost unbroken layer of white pumice."

"How do you know," the other asked, "that the missing sheet of blocks is not buried under the pumice?"

"Because," replied the Naturalist, "wherever we see the bottom of the pumice, as we do in the canyons around the lake, there is no trace of an underlying layer of blocks. Hundreds of pits have been dug through the pumice on the plateau east and northeast of here to find what there is below, and many wells have been drilled through the pumice in search of water. Everywhere, the pumice is found to lie on solid flows of lava, on glacial moraines, or on sand and gravel. It is certain that the missing top of Mount Mazama does not lie in fragments under the blanket of pumice."

"Then perhaps it is mixed with the pumice itself," interposed the other. "I mean, perhaps the mountain was shattered and hurled out in fragments at the same time as the pumice."

"Undoubtedly, some of the mountain was destroyed in that way," he answered. "But, all told, the amount of shattered rock mingled with the pumice amounts to slightly less than $1\frac{1}{2}$ cubic miles. Great though this volume is, don't forget that the volume of Mount Mazama which has disappeared is more than ten times greater."

"But isn't it possible that rivers have washed away a good deal of material?"

"No. Since Crater Lake was formed, the rivers have done no more than carve narrow canyons in the pumice."

"I am almost convinced," said the champion of the explosion theory, "but one more possibility occurs to me. Perhaps a large part of the mountaintop was pulverized to fine dust and carried for hundreds or even thousands of miles by the wind. Wouldn't it be practically impossible to estimate how much was lost in such a case?"

"Naturally, some rock dust was lost in that way, but the amount can only have been quite small. When light, frothy pumice and fragments of old lava are blown out together, the lava chips, being heavier, tend to fall from the air first and closer to the source. The farther we go from Crater Lake, the fewer and smaller they become. Yet among all the materials carried by the winds and showered over the ground to a depth of 6 inches to 15 feet, the total amount of old rock fragments is only a seventh of a cubic mile. Surely you will admit that the amount of fine rock dust blown beyond the 6-inch line must be even less."

"Then the scarcity of old rock fragments explodes my idea of explosion," acknowledged the argumentative one, with a smile.

"Consider next the possibility that the interior of the volcano was dissolved from within," went on the Naturalist, "and that the mixed liquid was then blown out as pumice. Some geologists say that this is what happened at Katmai in Alaska in 1912, when a large caldera was produced in the summit of the volcano. Their evidence is that the pumice blown out by Katmai is full of partly dissolved fragments of the mountaintop. However, none of the pumice around Crater Lake contains such partly digested old rocks. Besides, the entire amount of pumice is much less than the volume of the mountain that has vanished."

"As far as I am concerned," said the other, expressing what we all felt, "you have ruled out the possibility of explosion; but I still fail to see how the mountain could have collapsed."

"To cause collapse," replied the Naturalist, "support must have been withdrawn from under the top of the mountain by removal of liquid magma from a feeding chamber below. Dr. Diller, the first geologist to study Crater Lake, knew that at the famous 'fire pit' of Kilauea, in Hawaii, the walls often collapse when lava pours from cracks far down the sides of the volcano and so is drained from beneath the floor of the pit. He felt sure that the top of Mount Mazama must have been engulfed in the same way. Yet he searched in vain for lavas that might have poured from fractures around the base of the mountain."

"Has anyone else looked for them?"

"Yes, but without success. I think we can safely say that it was not the drainage of the chamber under Mount Mazama by an outpouring of lava on the surface that brought about collapse. I put the question to you, How else might the chamber have been sufficiently emptied?"

One member of the party suggested that the pumice eruptions must have removed a vast amount of liquid from inside the volcano; another, that cracks might have opened deep down and been filled with magma without any surface eruptions.

"If we combine your answers," the Naturalist said, "we shall have solved most of the mystery. It was by a combination of both processes that the reservoir was drained. Let me explain. Apart from the fragments of old lava torn from the summit of the volcano, between 12 and 15 cubic miles of material were deposited around Crater Lake by the pumice fall and glowing avalanches. This does not mean, however, that this volume of liquid magma was blown from the reservoir. Between 2 and 3.5 cubic miles of the material consists of crystals; the rest of it is

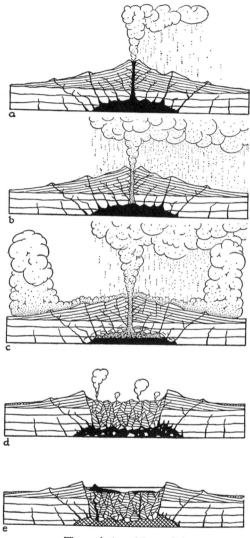

The evolution of Crater Lake.

a. Beginning of the great eruptions.

b. Eruptions become more violent and pumice showers heavier. Lava level in pipe is falling.

c. Climax of the eruptions. Glowing avalanches sweep down the sides of the volcano. Magma chamber is being rapidly drained.

d. Summit collapses into magma chamber. Gas vents appear in the caldera floor.

e. Crater Lake today. Wizard Island and lava are shown on the lake floor. Magma in underlying chamber is in large part, or entirely, solidified.

frothy volcanic glass or pumice. If all this frothy glass were remelted to liquid, the volume would be reduced to between 4 and 7 cubic miles. In other words, 7 or 8 cubic miles of magma were actually blown from the reservoir, including between 4 and 7 of liquid that frothed into pumice and 2 to 3.5 of crystals floating in the liquid. The eruptions were so rapid that the reservoir couldn't have refilled at a comparable rate. Hence, about 7 or 8 cubic miles of the mountaintop must have collapsed to replace the magma erupted."

At last we were beginning to see the light. "We still have almost as much more of the mountain to account for," he continued, "and only one explanation is left. Large volumes of liquid must have been drained from the reservoir by the opening of cracks at greath depth. Most probably, swarms of cracks opened parallel to the axis of the Cascade Range and were filled at once with magma. Don't think this is just an idle guess, because in many parts of the world where volcanoes have been deeply eroded we find the underlying rocks cut by a maze of cracks filled with solidified magma. The history of Kilauea and Mauna Loa in Hawaii tells us that, deep beneath those volcanoes, wide-stretching fissures are opened repeatedly. In fact, the record of most volcanoes shows that long and gradual rise of lava from below is usually ended by sudden withdrawals suggestive of drainage far underground."

"Would you mind summarizing the figures you just gave us?"

—*Photo Air Corps, U.S. Army*

DUTTON CLIFF AND PHANTOM SHIP. THE TRIANGULAR CLIFF JUST BELOW THE
CENTER OF THE PICTURE IS THE FILLING OF A VOLCANIC PIPE

—*Photo National Park Service*

REDCLOUD CLIFF

—*Photo National Park Service*

Dutton Cliff, Phantom Ship, and Sun Notch, as Seen from Near Kerr Notch

—*Photo National Park Service*

The Pinnacles, Sand Creek Canyon

"Not at all," he replied. "I can express the conclusion most simply this way. Approximately one-tenth of the vanished top of Mount Mazama was blown away in fragments; the remaining nine-tenths collapsed into the underlying reservoir when it was suddenly drained by eruptions of pumice at the surface and by escape of magma into cracks deep below."

"How quickly do you think the collapse occurred?" we asked.

"We can only speculate," he answered. "From analogy with what happens at other volcanoes, we would judge that the whole catastrophe may have lasted only a few days."

He apologized for continuing at such length, but we urged him on. "There is one more feature about the collapse that I should like to mention," he said. "The middle of Crater Lake does not lie straight down from the original top of the mountain. In other words, the collapse was eccentric."

"How on earth can you tell?"

"Because, if you will recall, the north wall of Crater Lake is much lower than the south wall."

"Can you give us a simple explanation?" he was asked.

"You will remember from your boat trip around the lake," he responded, "that the feeding pipes of many of the lavas, such as those of Llao Rock, Cleetwood Cove, and Redcloud, lie on the northern half of the caldera wall. Obviously, that cannot be simply a coincidence. The pipes lie on a semicircular crack, and it was the existence of this line of weakness that caused more of the mountain to collapse on the north side of the summit than on the south."

"May we trouble you to answer one more question?"

He kindly assented, and the speaker asked, "Are there any other calderas in the world that were formed in the same way as Crater Lake?"

"Yes," he replied. "In fact, nowadays volcanologists are generally agreed that all calderas are produced by collapse of the tops of volcanoes following rapid evacuation of the feeding chambers. Explosions by themselves rarely form cavities more than a mile across. Let me give you one example of a volcano that met the same fate as Mount Mazama. Doubtless many of you have heard of the celebrated volcano of Krakatoa in the East Indies. The eruptions that brought about its collapse blew so much fine dust into the upper atmosphere that for years afterward there were brilliant sunsets all over the world.

"For more than two centuries Krakatoa had been quiet. In May, 1883, mild eruptions of pumice began, like those which marked the opening activity at Mount Mazama. The eruptions continued at intervals for three months. On August 26th and 27th they reached a climax. On those two fateful days tremendous outbursts of pumice occurred, like those which formed the glowing avalanches from Mazama. A column of steam and dust rose 17 miles into the air and the noise of the explosions was heard 2000 miles away. Accompanying the eruptions, there were devastating tidal waves. On the adjacent shores of Java and Sumatra, 36,000 natives were drowned. When the climax